CAPE HATTERAS

AMERICA'S LIGHTHOUSE

CAPE HATTERAS
AMERICA'S LIGHTHOUSE

THOMAS YOCUM, BRUCE ROBERTS,
AND CHERYL SHELTON-ROBERTS

CUMBERLAND HOUSE
NASHVILLE, TENNESSEE

Published by Cumberland House Publishing, Inc., 431 Harding Industrial Drive, Nashville, Tennessee 37211.

Cover design by Bateman Design, Inc., Nashville, Tennessee.

Library of Congress Cataloging-in-Publication Data

Yocum, Thomas, 1960–
    Cape Hatteras : America's lighthouse / Thomas Yocum, Bruce Roberts, and Cheryl Shelton-Roberts.
      p. cm.
    Includes bibliographical references and index.
    ISBN 1-58182-032-1 (pbk. : alk. paper)
    ISBN 1-58182-033-X (hc. : alk. paper)
    1. Cape Hatteras Lighthouse (N.C.) I. Roberts, Bruce, 1930– . II. Shelton-Roberts, Cheryl, 1950– . III. Title.
VK1025.C27Y63 1999
387.1'55'09756175—dc21
                                           99-31039
                                            CIP

Printed in the United States of America.

1 2 3 4 5 6 7 8—03 02 01 00 99

To Janet and Charles Yocum, who taught Thomas to love the
Cape Hatteras Lighthouse
To Dexter Stetson, the man who built the lighthouse
To Courtney Adelaide Whisler, Cheryl's young
and prodigious beacon

CONTENTS

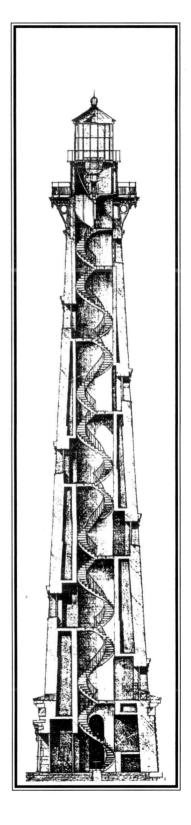

PREFACE

THE CAPE HATTERAS LIGHTHOUSE is the most recognized, photographed, painted, visited, read about, and admired lighthouse in North America. It is the signature of our maritime history. It is a symbol of the U.S. Lighthouse Service and a memorial to the hundreds of caring professional men and women who made this dangerous coastline safer for mariners. It is the signpost of the Graveyard of the Atlantic. It is the gnomon of the earth's sundial casting shadows on the places of rest for those making the journey in these tricky waters.

This sentinel is an awe-inspiring structure of architectural beauty. It has endured for 130 years and has defied the elements while a formidable opponent, Mother Nature, has fought to reclaim her own.

Writers have waxed poetic in millions of words about this lighthouse, this guardian of the sea. Artists have painted its image in every medium known to man; however, its meaning today is revealed in the following letter written by a member of the Outer Banks Lighthouse Society:

> My family has been going to the Outer Banks since 1950 and things have changed quite a bit since then. Everything except the Hatteras Light—it's always there. Now that I have a family that is grown, we carry on a tradition that started in 1954 with my father.
>
> From our home in Ohio it takes 12 hours to reach the Banks. We always leave about 5:00 P.M. so we can arrive about 5:00 A.M. just to see the light. As we leave Avon toward Buxton it's with us all the way toward our second home (in our hearts).
>
> The walls in my living room are covered with pictures and prints of the light collected for decades.
>
> From the beach at Hatteras village, we can see the ever-steady beam of the light. To us, it's much more than brick, stone, and steel. It's a steady, comforting beam that says, "All's well. Good night."

The majority of such admirers can only dream of visiting the esteemed sentinel. Marion McNally Roberts, my mother-in-law, was born in Canada and raised in New York and had never visited the Cape Hatteras Lighthouse. Imagine our surprise when her will requested that her ashes be scattered off the coast near the tower.

The Cape Hatteras Lighthouse embodies the romance associated with these structures that crown the land that they guard. There is no record of how many people have become engaged at the Hatteras Lighthouse. However, volunteers who stand at the tower entry tell us that a couple can enter looking indistinguishable from other visitors, but when they descend and exit the lighthouse, there is an unmistakable indication that something special happened at the summit of this tower. "They float down," volunteer Jean Simmons says with delight.

Volunteer Mary Dickens's favorite lighthouse story begins, "The first weekend in November 1998, Bob May and I were at the top of the tower and Betty May was at the bottom. Betty came to us quickly and said, 'If you see a bunch of people down on the ground scrambling around, pay no attention.' A couple had climbed to the top of the lighthouse to become engaged. The young man knelt before his bride-to-be, reached into his pocket, brought out a jeweler's box, and opened it. The ring had come out of the center slot and a gust of wind swept it over the railing of the tower and all the way down to the sand! Now, we aren't talking an insignificant ring," Mary continues. "This was a *rock!* The bride was weeping all the way down the stairway fearing that the ring was gone forever. The groom quickly enlisted as many visitors as possible to search for the engagement ring by scooping down several inches into the sand all around the tower. And a gentleman scooped down deep, about four or five inches, and came up with the ring on one of his fingers! Bob and I hadn't seen the couple before they lost the ring, but we knew them right away as they stepped through the door at the top of the tower the second time in the 'greatest of clinches.' The young woman was crying, tears streaming down her face. They were hugging and kissing and looking beyond joy. He led his bride-to-be to the very same spot and gave her the ring and proposed."

Tucked away in many photo albums are wedding pictures taken at the Cape Hatteras Lighthouse. One special ceremony took place on a beautiful sunny afternoon on the northeast side of the principal keepers house. On that day Rany Jennette, the son of the last keeper, married lighthouse volunteer Lynn O'Neal. The tower served as a dramatic backdrop for this happy event. Rany is one of the rare links to the daily life that had surrounded the last family to live in the shadow of the Cape Hatteras Light Station. His father, Unaka Jennette, was the revered Capt'n 'Naka, the principal keeper from 1919 until the station closed in 1936. Rany has shared his memories of the lighthouse and its importance as a guide for sailors. He knows as well as anyone the importance of this lighthouse not only as a historic landmark but also as a navigational landmark.

Hatteras sits on the edge of the continent marking the line between sand and water, safety and danger. This light station site has witnessed all that has come to pass since the birth of this nation until the present. Its history is our history.

Hatteras affords intriguing insights into much of America's maritime heritage. But today's view of the charming way of island life obscures the truth of the "bankers'" struggle for survival by herring seine and shad boat fishing, of the work given by dedicated lighthouse keepers and lifesaving service surfmen. Scores of original islanders were lost to cholera, typhoid, "brain fever," "typhoid pneumonia," diarrhea, and "lung fever." The ability to live on the Outer Banks was born of sheer determination.

The same attraction that makes the subject of lighthouses popular is also true of the Cape Hatteras Light Station: There will always be more to learn. Valuable Lighthouse Service documents were destroyed in a fire in the Department of Commerce in 1920, and priceless artifacts were lost during the absorption of the Lighthouse Service by the U.S. Coast Guard in 1939 as America prepared for a world war. Today no one knows where the log books (books with daily entries of weather and significant events at the light station) are or if they even exist.

In the records we do have, mariners' accounts from centuries ago name Cape Hatteras as one of the most dreaded places of passage. For southbound ships to get around Cape Hatteras more quickly in the southerly flow of a cold current, the trick was to find the deep water between the northerly flow of the warm Gulf Stream and Diamond Shoals, offshore ridges of sand that could stop a vessel dead in its tracks. And here nature often played tricks, deadly ones.

When these two courses of opposing waters wander into one another, unpredictable weather results. Here are born the notoriously sudden and violent storms, the blinding fog that leaves the mariner disoriented, the baneful hurricanes whose winds are driven by the warm gulf waters, and the furious nor'easters drawn into the area by the lie of the land. Rounding Cape Hatteras in any weather always threatened a ship with being driven into Diamond Shoals.

Moving the Cape Hatteras Light Station into the future, experts prepared meticulously to lift the tower and place it on a new foundation about sixteen hundred feet from the ocean. The scientific, environmental, and lighthouse communities applauded the hard-earned efforts for relocation. The moving of this sentinel affirms a national commitment to restore and preserve America's heritage for future generations to experience.

The Cape Hatteras Lighthouse remains a major aid to navigation after its relocation, and it also serves as a memorial to the thousands of keepers and their families as well as other dedicated U.S. Lighthouse Service personnel. They ran personal marathons to keep a light in the tower. As North Carolina's strongest symbol and as a memorial to the Lighthouse Service, the Cape Hatteras Lighthouse is inspiration to young and old alike to continue doing one's best even in the harshest of conditions.

A lighthouse volunteer shares a story that witnesses the transition of a man-made structure beyond bricks and mortar for those who come to pay homage:

For many years a couple came to climb the Cape Hatteras Lighthouse. As the years passed and age set in, the climbing became a bit more difficult for them. One year the old gentleman came alone after his wife had passed away. He left a rose at the lighthouse for her each year he continued to visit and climb. As time passed he too became infirm and found it difficult to come alone, so he was brought to Cape Hatteras by his son. Together they would leave a rose, symbolic of their appreciation for this sentinel and in honor of their wife and mother. Recently the son was seen visiting the Cape Hatteras Lighthouse.

He came alone.

He left two roses.

Cheryl Shelton-Roberts

ACKNOWLEDGMENTS

In WRITING ANY BOOK there are unsung heroes who contribute in various but important ways to help a book become reality. The following are those to whom we want to express our sincerest appreciation.

Thanks to Norma McKittrick for help in editing portions of this book as well as to Joe Jakubik of International Chimney Corporation and Dr. Stanley Riggs of East Carolina University, professor of coastal geology, who added quotes and other comments according to their fields of expertise. We want to recognize Bill Parrish, who wrote hundreds of letters and kept the authors apprised of media coverage on the progress toward relocation appropriations. Without the help of Sen. Lauch Faircloth and his chief legal council, Sean Callinicos, Congress might never have funded the relocation process. Thanks also to Tim Harrison of *Lighthouse Digest* who pledged unfailing support, advising us on portions of this book and writing his comments for it.

Cullen Chambers, restoration expert at Tybee Island Light Station in Georgia, offered support and ever-ready technical advice. Dr. Orrin Pilkey of Duke University, a coastal geologist, has been gracious in allowing use of diagrams from his most recent book on the development of barrier islands.

Charlie Votaw helped consolidate National Park Service (NPS) databases of keepers at Hatteras. NPS chief of resource management Steve Harrison, NPS chief of planning and partnerships Bob Woody, NPS superintendent Bob Reynolds, NPS former superintendent Russell Berry, Cape Hatteras historian Rob Bolling, and Andrew Kling all contributed tremendous help in research and finding answers to our questions. Volunteers Mary Dickens and Jean Simmons shared wonderful stories about visitors to the light station.

We are also indebted to the staffs of both the Cape Hatteras National Seashore and the Outer Banks History Center for their assistance in assembling the many small bits and pieces of information that helped put together the complete story of the Cape Hatteras Lighthouse. Both facilities, just west of the northern Outer Banks on Roanoke Island, offer an array of information available nowhere else.

We would especially like to thank the knowledgeable Wynne Dough, Sarah Downing, and Brian Edwards at the Outer Banks History Center, a library with excellent information and pictures of the Cape Hatteras Light Station. Through the foresight of Outer Banks historian David Stick, this research facility is now a reality. David's half-century of research and writing have provided a framework for all subsequent work on the history of the area. He is the foremost historian of the Outer Banks, and the gift of his entire collection of papers, maps, and books to the history center in Manteo will ensure that much information that would be otherwise lost will be available to future generations.

When researchers want to find historic information on the Cape Hatteras Light Station and the light vessels of Diamond Shoals, they inevitably acquaint themselves with the in-depth report that F. Ross Holland Jr. submitted in 1968 on the light station and the structure report for the keepers dwelling. Holland's report for the National Park Service stands alone as the definitive overview of the history of the three lighthouses at Hatteras. He completed a thirty-year career with the National Park Service beginning as a park historian in California and concluding with numerous meritorious awards for his contributions to historic preservation. Holland served on the 1987 National Academy of Sciences Committee and was a strong voice recommending relocation. He thought it better to retain the tower in something like its original setting rather than surround it with a sea wall as the point eroded and allow the lighthouse to became an isolated offshore monument. The authors gratefully acknowledge his contributions to the preservation of all of America's lighthouses and their history.

An understanding of the history of the Outer Banks and the lighthouses that have safeguarded them would be impossible without the efforts of either of these two men—David Stick and F. Ross Holland Jr. Abundant thanks are also tendered to David for his help in editing the manuscript.

Others affording help with specific topics are Steve Messengill at the North Carolina Department of Archives and History; Nelson Morosini of Pigeon Point Light Station, Año Nuevo State Reserve, Pescadero, California; Candace Clifford and Ralph E. Eshelman of Maritime Initiative, Department of the Interior; NPS for information on the declaration of Cape Hatteras as a National Historic Landmark; Jim Claflin, an antiquarian who helped with the search for archival material on Cape Hatteras; and Mike Litwin, who did the artist's renderings for this book. A hearty thank you to Thomas Tag, America's leading expert on lighthouse lamp apparatus sys-

The 1870 Cape Hatteras Lighthouse was designed and built during the heyday of new American lights following the Civil War. Many damaged southern towers were rebuilt at this time, and around the country, new lights were erected and strategically situated to make U.S. coasts and lakeshores the best marked in the world. When the work on the lighthouse at Hatteras began in 1868, its builders integrated the most advanced engineering techniques of their day with a decorative design and utilized the finest materials available.

tems and lenses, for reviewing and enriching the information on the Fresnel lens and for his image and information on the incandescent oil vapor (IOV) lamp. Another expert in the modern-day field of lighting lighthouses is MKC Nicholas Johnston, command chief, U.S. Coast Guard Group at Fort Macon, who offered valuable data. We gratefully acknowledge videographer Kevin Duffus for giving us the lead on the burial site for Dexter Stetson. We received valuable assistance from Sandy Clunies, a certified genealogist who has done extensive research into Record Group 26 in the National Archives, which hold the extant records of the U.S. Lighthouse Service and the U.S. Coast Guard. She recently verified that Stetson oversaw the construction of the Currituck Beach Lighthouse in 1875 after he had completed both the Hatteras and Bodie Island Lighthouses in 1870 and 1872, respectively. Our special thanks is also due to Carol Phelps of the Auburn Public Library, Maine, for discovering the portrait engraving of Stetson reproduced in this book on page 49. And a thank you to all who believe in this light station as one of our nation's greatest maritime symbols and who have inspired our endeavors.

Finally, preparation of this book would not have been possible without the kindness and generosity of others. We would like to thank Jeannie and Jeremie Berube of Arundel, Maine, and Mike and Anne Wardwell Sayre of Canaan Valley, West Virginia, for providing Thomas with a perfect place to prepare this book, and his two dear friends, Amy Smith and Mary Anna La Fratta, for all of their support and encouragement throughout the entire process.

INTRODUCTION

Cape hatteras. for centuries the name has sent a shiver down the spines of the most seasoned sailors. It's a place where currents collide and winds howl and the bottom rises out of the sea to form a maze of sifting shoals extending more than fifteen miles into the Atlantic. It's a place where more than six hundred ships have met their match and gone to a watery tomb in the "Graveyard of the Atlantic." And it's a place where for more than two hundred years Americans have struggled to mark the edge of the continent with a lighthouse to guide mariners to safety.

This is the story of that struggle and of the progress and pitfalls placed in the path of those who worked to build and operate the light stations at Cape Hatteras. There were three. The first was erected in 1803, but it was too low and its light too dim. A second was built in 1870 and has stood at its post for 129 years. A third light tower was erected in 1935.

Almost from the start, the nature of the Outer Banks seemed to fight the efforts to harness its dangers. Wind scoured the sand from the base of the first lighthouse, exposing its foundation and weakening the tower. Hurricanes and nor'easters hammered the lantern, breaking windows and damaging the delicate lighting equipment inside. The ocean has threatened to topple the second light, leading the Lighthouse Service in the 1930s to abandon the tower and erect a third lighthouse on a small hill safely inland. For fifteen years the 1870 tower was dark. Vandals frequently attacked the light, smashing windows and doors and destroying the lens. After significant renovations, the black-and-white striped tower was relighted in 1950.

In the nearly half-century since the 1870 Cape Hatteras Lighthouse has again been operating, there have been new dangers. The sea has again advanced and in the 1990s was within a hundred feet of the base of the tower. Two decades of debate about how to protect the tower concluded with a decision to move the lighthouse sixteen hundred feet to a site that will again place it a little more than a quarter of a mile from the shore, the same distance it was when it was completed in 1870.

For years the most uniquely decorated cottage in Nags Head was the Fearing Cottage. Its owner had collected nameplates from wrecked ships all along the Outer Banks and nailed them to his house on the sound near Jockeys Ridge. The cottage is no longer standing, but the nameplates from these once-proud ships were removed to the Chicamacomico Lifesaving Station.

Advancements in technology also threatened the lighthouse. Improvements such as global positioning satellites have eliminated the need for lighthouses, changing the role of the Cape Hatteras Lighthouse and dozens of other lighthouses around the country, leaving them with shrinking budgets for vital repairs and maintenance.

Yet despite the changing nature of the sea and technology, the future of the Hatteras light seems bright. Each year more than a quarter million people visit the Hatteras light, climbing the 268 steps to the top of the tower for an unparalleled view of Hatteras Island, Cape Hatteras, and the dreaded Diamond Shoals. They climb the same steps the keepers of the lighthouse did as they tended the beacons for nearly 130 years, looking out over the same landscape and the same turbulent weather and water that has claimed scores of lives.

For these new keepers of the Cape Hatteras Lighthouse, the flashing white light may no longer mean life or death to sailors at sea, but it still means something. What was once a warning to mariners is now a monument to the technology and workmanship of the men who built it. It's a testament to more than two hundred years of struggle and progress that helped shape the future of the country and chart the course of the world. It's about a place called Cape Hatteras and about the lighthouse that still shines there.

Thomas Yocum

CAPE HATTERAS

AMERICA'S LIGHTHOUSE

PART 1

THE DEARBORN TOWER

I

THE FIRST
LIGHTHOUSE

THE STONE GUARDIAN BY THE SEA

> *[A lighthouse] on some part of Cape Hatteras, would be an establishment of very great utility to the navigation of the United States.*
>
> ALEXANDER HAMILTON

SINCE THE FIRST EUROPEAN explorers traveled along the North Caro-lina coast, Cape Hatteras has been on the map. Forming a pro-nounced bend in the barrier island chain known as the Outer Banks, the cape is a shoal-marked finger of sand where land and sea come together.

Formed in part by the collision of two powerful ocean cur-rents—the Gulf Stream and the Virginia Coastal Current—the low sandy bottom often lies barely hidden beneath the waves. East of Cape Hatteras lie the treacherous Diamond Shoals, fourteen miles of shifting sand and deadly currents that have claimed hundreds of ships and thousands of lives in an area that has become known as the Graveyard of the Atlantic.

Early sailing-ship captains had no choice but to round the cape and its treacherous shoals as they traveled along the east coast of North America. Northbound ships took advantage of the swift-moving waters of the Gulf Stream and the prevailing southwest winds. With currents pulling the ships along at speeds of more than four knots, riding the Gulf Stream could cut weeks off a northerly journey home for the Europeans. Southbound ships

The turbulent waters off Cape Hatteras have been called the Graveyard of the Atlantic. Mariners have never known what to expect when entering this area of the Atlantic with its ever-changing currents, shoals, and weather. David Stick, one of the leading historians of the Outer Banks, wrote, "I have looked at the sea a thousand times, from the same spot and through the same eyes, and I have seen a thousand different seas."

faced a more daunting challenge. These captains had to thread a navigational needle, keeping the Gulf Stream to their left and Diamond Shoals to their right as they rounded the cape. If everything went well and the weather cooperated, the passage was accomplished uneventfully. But things often did not go as planned.

Traveling at the mercy of the wind, southbound ships had to wait for the wind to blow from the right direction before they could round the cape. Often storms arrived first, shredding sails, snapping spars, and driving the helpless ships onto the shoals. "The whole ocean shore of North Carolina is a terror to navigators, and is noted for the number of shipwrecks, especially near Cape Hatteras," wrote Edmund Ruffin, a prominent journalist of the mid-nineteenth century.

By the early 1700s colonial merchants had tired of their losses due to preventable shipwrecks. Failing to find support from the British crown, they collaborated to solve the problem themselves. Thus, as a first step, in 1715 Massachusetts merchants funded the building of a lighthouse on Little Brewster Island in Boston Harbor to help guide ships into port.

In that same year North Carolina officials also took the first steps to improve their commercial maritime interests, but they faced a more difficult challenge. Although the three-hundred-mile North Carolina coast constituted more than a quarter of the colonial seaboard, the state lacked any significant deep-water ports. Instead, the mainland was flanked on the east by the low-slung barrier islands, an obstacle that could only be cleared by navigating the often turbulent waters of the Outer Banks inlets.

As a result, North Carolina officials stationed ship pilots familiar with the shifting shoals and channels in the inlets at the vital points along the coast. The pilots boarded inbound ships and guided them safely to the colony's mainland harbors. Rudimentary channel markers and buoys were also put into place, although frequent storms regularly blew the markers away. The cost of these navigational improvements was borne by levies assessed on the incoming cargoes.

Although the pilots and navigational aids helped reduce some of the risks involved with sailing the Carolina coast, increasing trade led to an increasing number of wrecks and mounting losses for the merchants. By the end of the American Revolution, when the ports of the new nation were again opened to the world, it was clear something more needed to be done.

During the late 1700s, North Carolina's principal ports of entry were Ocracoke Inlet, Beaufort Inlet, and the Cape Fear River. In 1784 the state secured land at the mouth of the Cape Fear for the construction of a lighthouse. Five years later, in 1789, private citizens moved to build a lighthouse at Shell Castle Island in the middle of Ocracoke Inlet.

Another "tombstone" in the Graveyard of the Atlantic. The *Laura A. Barnes* wrecked on June 1, 1921, on Bodie Island, forty miles north of Hatteras, but no lives were lost. The bones of this old ship may still be viewed in the Cape Hatteras National Seashore at Coquina Beach, near the Bodie Island lighthouse. Following hurricanes and strong nor'easters, other remains of shipwrecks are uncovered by the shifting sands, giving a glimpse of what the waters of the Graveyard of the Atlantic hold in abundance from storms past. Northbound sailing ships often lay off the coast of Hatteras to wait for prevailing winds and currents to speed their course. Unfortunately, the scenario often involved raucous weather, which sent many a sailor down with his ship.

At about the same time, the fledgling federal government was also turning its attention to the problems facing maritime trade. President George Washington saw the rich potential of America's merchant fleet and the need to safeguard commercial shipping, but it was Alexander Hamilton, the first secretary of the treasury, who played the fundamental role in the development of the country's lighthouses and other navigational aids.

Years earlier, seventeen-year-old Hamilton had been en route to Boston from the West Indies when the ship on which he was sailing—the *Thunderbolt*—caught fire and came close to sinking off Cape Hatteras in 1772. Hamilton was almost killed, and the incident made a lasting impression on the future statesman. He called the dreaded area off Hatteras the "Graveyard of the Atlantic" and determined to do something about the mounting number of ships lost there.

In 1789 Hamilton gained congressional approval of a lighthouse bill, which placed the nascent government at the forefront of the worldwide efforts to improve maritime safety. The legislation transferred all lands and lighthouses and their maintenance and operation to the Treasury Department and also created the Revenue Cutter Service, the forerunner to the U.S. Coast Guard. With the new bill in hand, one of the first orders of business for Hamilton was Cape Hatteras.

In August 1789 Hamilton was authorized to investigate the feasibility of constructing a lighthouse on the cape. The new United States had no such lighthouses at the time, only beacons marking harbors and channels. Lighthouses had never been constructed to warn mariners *away* from land.

The constant cry from merchants and captains, however, could not be ignored. Hamilton directed Tench Coxe, the commissioner of revenue responsible for the Treasury Department's aids to navigation, to determine what was necessary to improve the navigation along the Carolina coast. Coxe responded with a recommendation to construct a substantial lighthouse at Cape Hatteras and a smaller beacon to guide ships at Ocracoke Inlet. Hamilton concurred, and in 1794 Congress authorized both the Ocracoke beacon and a lighthouse of "the first rate" for Hatteras.

Coxe was next charged with finding suitable land and a contractor for the twin projects. Neither task was simple. North Carolina officials had also been working to secure land for the construction of a lighthouse at Cape Hatteras. Although state offi-

---

The waters off Cape Hatteras have generated many strange tales over the years but perhaps none more intriguing than that of the fate of twenty-nine-year-old Theodosia Burr Alston, wife of Gov. John Alston and daughter of former Vice President Aaron Burr.

She was traveling aboard the schooner *Patriot* when it left Georgetown, South Carolina, for New York on December 30, 1812. The *Patriot* never arrived, and a subsequent investigation turned up nothing, except that a violent storm had moved across the Outer Banks at about the time the ship would have been rounding Cape Hatteras.

Assuming the ship had been lost due to weather, family members grieved for those aboard. Twenty years later and a thousand miles away, new information exposed a startling story.

In 1833 an Alabama man confessed on his deathbed that he had helped capture the *Patriot,* killing those on board and scuttling the ship to hide the evidence. In 1848 another man confessed to being part of the same plot, adding that one of the passengers was named "Odessa Burr Alston," and that she had chosen death rather than surrender to the amorous alternative offered by the captain. Then, in 1869, the notorious

pirate captain in question, Dominique You, allegedly confessed to the crime.

That same year a doctor who vacationed on the Outer Banks was called to treat an elderly woman who was ill. On the wall of her cabin was the portrait of a young woman, which had obviously been painted by a professional and which struck the doctor as totally out of keeping with the sparse decor of the little cabin in which the old woman lived.

The doctor refused to bill the woman so she instead gave him the portrait he had commented upon, saying it came from a deserted vessel that rode ashore with its sails set one winter morning long ago when "we were fighting the British."

The doctor took the portrait home to Elizabeth City, North Carolina, thinking little more about the portrait or what the old woman had told him until friends remarked that the young woman in the portrait bore a striking resemblance to members of the Burr family. When a family member arrived at the doctor's home to see the portrait for herself, she was shocked to find a likeness that bore an uncanny resemblance to her sister.

cials cooperated with the federal move to assume responsibility for the construction and maintenance of the lighthouse on the cape, complications with the land transfer consumed valuable time. When Coxe finally succeeded in securing the property transfer, the three-year limit on the legislation authorizing his efforts had expired, and he had to begin the process all over again.

Finding a contractor for such far-flung construction work was no easier. Local builders and craftsmen had little interest in the project, so Coxe placed notices throughout the country calling for suitable candidates. The results were not encouraging. Coxe deemed the first bid he received as "dishonest and impudent" and filled with "misconceptions and misinterpretations." A second contractor offered to erect just the Cape Hatteras light for more than double the amount appropriated for both beacons.

Coxe finally contacted John McComb, a brick mason who had built the Montauk Point and Cape Henry Lighthouses, agreeing to pay him $37,500 to erect the Hatteras light alone. McComb accepted the offer, but construction was delayed during renegotiations for the property, and McComb turned his attention elsewhere.

By the summer of 1797, Coxe had again secured the necessary land for the lighthouse at Cape Hatteras. In July, Henry Dearborn, a two-term Massachusetts congressman for whom the Michigan city was named, contacted Coxe and said he might be interested in building the Hatteras and Shell Castle lights. Coxe received Dearborn's bid, along with two others, and forwarded them to President John Adams for review. Confident that Dearborn would be selected, Coxe ordered the purchase of the property for the two new beacons for the Outer Banks. Just as it appeared the projects were moving forward, another obstacle arose.

Before Adams could approve the construction contract, Coxe was replaced as commissioner of revenue. His successor, William Miller Jr., thought the Dearborn bid lacked specific breakdowns, especially in the areas of materials and transportation costs. Miller asked Adams to decline Dearborn's proposal, which the president did. Then Miller eliminated what he construed as vague wordings from the contract and contacted Dearborn and McComb, inviting them to submit revised bids for the lighthouse construction. Apparently McComb was no longer interested, but Dearborn responded favorably. It took a year for him to draft and submit a contract that met with Miller's approval. By the end of October 1798 the contract was finally signed.

Dearborn agreed to build both the Cape Hatteras lighthouse and the Ocracoke beacon for $38,450, payable in five installments as the work progressed. According to the final contract,

The 1803 lighthouse light was generated by a number of lamps and reflectors that had to be lighted and cleaned individually. For decades ship captains complained about the poor quality of the light.

the construction at Cape Hatteras included an octagonal stone tower 90 feet tall and a 12-foot lantern, an oil vault and shed, and a two-story frame dwelling 34 feet long and 16 feet wide.

In November 1798 Dearborn requested and received an $8,000 advance to purchase materials. He acquired the sandstone that would be used to erect the tower from a New Hampshire quarry, and by the spring of 1799 he departed for Hatteras by sea. It was not long before more obstacles hindered the completion of his task.

En route to the Outer Banks, Dearborn's ship developed problems and had to put in at Boston, where repair delays stretched on for weeks. Finally, in late August, Dearborn, his men, and the building materials arrived at Ocracoke Inlet.

Dearborn made a quick survey of what was needed to construct the wooden beacon at Shell Castle and then sailed up Pamlico Sound to a point close to where the Hatteras lighthouse was to be built. It was more than a mile to the construction site from the soundside landing where Dearborn's vessel docked, a distance over which all the materials for the new light station would have to be carried. At the least the sandy, sometimes marshy route made transportation difficult. Wooden tracks were placed over the worst sections. Teams of oxen pulled the carts of equipment to the construction site.

When Dearborn and his men finally arrived, the area around the lighthouse site appeared much different than it does today. A small wooded ridge rose above the island, ending abruptly and creating a small headland where the tower was to be built. The four-acre site, which had been purchased for $50, was covered with live oak, holly, cedar, and dogwood trees. Preliminary surveys had recommended that the contractor retain as much of the wooded cover as possible when he built the tower. Disturbing the sand hills too much could trigger wind erosion, engineers warned. It was a farsighted prediction.

Dearborn's most immediate concern was housing his crew, and work began on the keepers quarters, which would also serve as the crew quarters for the construction project. It was a spartan, wood-frame structure designed to meet very simple needs. When the quarters were completed, Dearborn returned to Ocracoke Island to meet with an inspector, Samuel Tredwell, the customs collector from Edenton, North Carolina, and to begin the work on the Shell Castle beacon.

The late summer weather cooperated, and by October the project had advanced to the point where Dearborn received his second contract allocation of $2,000. He received his third allocation—$4,000—in December, at which point he suspended work until spring and sent his crew home.

In March 1800, Dearborn assembled another construction crew and returned to the Outer Banks. These workers prepared a foundation for the tower by excavating a hole ten feet deep to reach hard, compacted sand. They then constructed a stone foundation bound together with mortar made from local oyster-shell lime.

The quality of the foundation is open to debate. Customs collector Tredwell reported that it was of fine quality and met the specific requirements set forth in the contract. Engineering inspections seventy years later painted a much different picture of a poorly constructed foundation only a foot wider at the base than at the top.

By July 1800 the construction crew had raised the tower to the base of its second story. Dearborn received an additional $2,500, which brought the amount paid to roughly half the total contract amount. Although the work had progressed well to this point, suddenly Dearborn was beset with numerous delays. The first of these occurred when his men began to get sick.

The hot and humid conditions of Hatteras Island that summer had been conducive to the maturation of hordes of insects. As a result, Dearborn's crew likely battled malaria, and it was clear that the malaria was winning. A dozen workers were bedridden, and one died. Construction slowed to a halt. Dearborn himself fled the island, either on business or to escape the unhealthy conditions. Before he left, he placed Dudley Hobart, his assistant, in charge, but the continued illness among the crew soon forced Hobart to abandon the site. By the fall of 1800 work had again stopped on the tower.

Yet while construction ceased, Dearborn's debts from the project continued to mount. Although he had not yet met the contract requirements for additional allocations, he requested and received $5,500 before the end of 1800 and $3,000 in March 1801 before work resumed.

The work crews for the Hatteras project were again assembled in the spring of 1801. Again the tower steadily rose, and when the sweltering summer weather returned, so did the debilitating sickness among the crew. By August 1 they again abandoned the work site, leaving the tower far from complete and the treacherous cape unmarked for another year.

In 1861 Union troops captured the Hatteras lighthouse. Edwin Graves Champney was among them. He sketched a number of Outer Banks scenes, including this view of the first Cape Hatteras Lighthouse.

This photograph of the foundation of the Dearborn tower was taken in the 1960s. This area is now under water. The foundation itself was washed away in a winter storm in March 1980.

By this time, federal officials had become concerned with the slow progress in the lighthouse construction. They had given Dearborn more than $30,000 of a $38,500 contract, and while the work was nearing completion on the Shell Island beacon, the lighthouse at Cape Hatteras was far from finished.

Dearborn's men again returned to Hatteras Island in the spring of 1802. This time work proceeded well, and Hobart reported in June that the tower's masonry work had been completed and that all that remained to make both the lighthouse at Cape Hatteras and the beacon at Shell Castle operational were their lanterns. Hobart optimistically reported that he expected the beacons to be in service within a month, but delays again pushed that date back by more than a year. The shoals off Hatteras went unmarked for another stormy winter.

Finally, in the fall of 1803, more than nine years after the first federal authorization for the lighthouse project, a fixed white light flickered one hundred feet above the sands of Hatteras Island. Adam Gaskins was appointed as the first lighthouse keeper at a salary of $333 per year. He had waited a long time for the job. Gaskin had been appointed to the position by a friendly North Carolina congressman when the lighthouse had been authorized nine years before. His new duty took him 112 feet above sea level where he tended the eighteen whale-oil lamps that formed the beacon. Eighteen miles out at sea, for the first time in more than 275 years of European shipping, seafarers saw a tiny marker in the distance. Hamilton had his light.

2

1854
IMPROVEMENTS

THE LIGHTHOUSE GETS A LIFT

The light-houses, light-vessels, beacons and buoys and the accessories in the United States, are not as efficient as the interests of commerce, navigation and humanity demand.
1852 LIGHT-HOUSE BOARD REPORT

DEARBORN'S TOWER WAS BESET by problems from the outset. A combination of poor design and punishing Outer Banks weather demanded almost constant attention by the keeper and lighthouse officials.

Less than a year after the lighthouse became operational, it was apparent the 1,000-gallon capacity of the beacon's oil vaults was too small. The lighthouse was burning approximately 1,400 gallons of whale oil per year, so to meet the annual consumption needs, the oil capacity at the light station was doubled to 2,000 gallons.

The lighthouse lantern created its own share of problems. The heat generated by the eighteen open-flame lamps in the tiny lantern room was almost too much for the keeper to bear. On more than one occasion the keeper broke the room's window glass as he retreated from the sometimes unruly flames. An 1809 fire in the lantern room resulted in the loss of all the room's windows, putting the lighthouse out of commission for a short period of time.

The punishing weather of the Outer Banks also took its toll. A severe September gale in 1806 damaged the lantern and knocked

13

If you are confused about the different names used for the Lighthouse Service, there is reason. The various agencies responsible for America's lighthouses changed over time. There were three distinct periods of organization in the history of the Lighthouse Service. They were used during the corresponding time spans below and interchangeably throughout the lifetime of the service from 1789 to 1939.

1789–1852, U.S. Lighthouse Establishment (USLHE): The ninth law passed by the new federal Congress announced government responsibility for navigational aids. Revenue came from the general fund and financing from the Treasury Department, headed by Alexander Hamilton. Presidents George Washington, John Adams, and Thomas Jefferson personally approved lighthouse contracts and position appointments. In 1820 President James Monroe transferred lighthouse responsibilities to the fifth auditor of the treasury, Stephen Pleasonton. The frugal Pleasonton fostered dissatisfaction among the lighthouse keepers by allowing poor construction and refusing to replace inferior reflector lamp systems. Congress ordered an investigation of the service in 1851.

1852–1910, Light-House Board (Lighthouse Board): During a revolutionary time in lighthouse history, two senior naval officers, a junior naval officer, two army engineers, and a civilian scientist were appointed to evaluate the urgent need for improvement in America's lighthouse service. In 1852 these men became part of the nine-member Light-House Board. Immediately, Fresnel lenses were installed in lighthouses at critical sites and qualified lighthouse inspectors were appointed. New directives from the Light-House Board required that keepers be able to read and write, follow written procedures, and wear uniforms (1884). Before choosing a site for new construction, distances between lighthouses were considered. Day marks like the famous spirals at Hatteras were begun in the 1870s.

1910–1939, Bureau of Lighthouses: Military influence was removed from the Lighthouse Service except for one Army Corps of Engineers consultant. Cape Hatteras became part of the sixth lighthouse district (formerly fifth). In 1912 George R. Putnam, commissioner of lighthouses, implemented annual reports as a key avenue of communication from the administrators in Washington, D.C., to lighthouse keepers in remote locations. Putnam established a retirement system for field employees and kept the lighthouse service in the forefront of the latest technologies, including the use of radio beacons (1921) and radio range detection, electrification (late 1920s), and installing a national network of aerobeacons for night flying (1926–34).

Harold King, named commissioner in 1935, guided the lighthouse service into a merger with the U.S. Coast Guard in 1939 as America prepared for a second world war. King retired only six months after the merger. Today the Coast Guard is still responsible for all lighthouses used as navigational aids. Following the introduction of satellite positioning aids, however, many of these towers have been ceded to historical societies and other nonprofit groups.

out the beacon for more than a month. But fires, passing birds crashing into the glass, searing heat, and brutal weather were just part of the problems facing the Hatteras light. As time went by, a bigger concern presented itself: The lighthouse was not accomplishing the task for which it had been designed.

By 1806, less than three years after it was first lighted, the shortcomings of the Cape Hatteras Lighthouse were becoming obvious. Most importantly, the weak light of the lantern failed to reach across the fifteen miles of sea necessary to warn mariners of Diamond Shoals.

As a result, Congress appropriated funding for a survey of the shoals of three major capes of the Carolina coast—Cape Hatteras, Cape Lookout, and Cape Fear—to determine the feasibility of constructing a lighthouse at any or all of these points to give mariners better warnings while they were still in safe water. Thomas Coles and Jonathan Price, the principal surveyors for the project, concluded that the idea of placing lighthouses on the shoals themselves was not practical. The warning lights, they suggested, would have to come from shore and the lighthouse keepers would have to do their best to ensure that the beacons operated at their full potential. Unfortunately, such consistency was not always the case.

Throughout the early years of American lighthouse history, the men who served as keepers were often ill suited for the task. Many could neither read nor write. They had secured their positions through political connections rather than their own qualifications. As incompetent as some may have been, however, no keeper could expect to maintain his office if he permitted his light to go out. Such an offense was intolerable and often required an investigation and most likely the termination of the keeper's status.

For the keepers at Cape Hatteras, the light's position on one of the busiest sea lanes in the hemisphere made the slightest mistakes painfully obvious to every ship struggling to round the treacherous bend in the North Carolina coast. The keepers became a favorite target of captains who wanted to lessen their own liability with underwriters and clients. Some of these allegations may have been properly directed, but there were plenty of shipmasters who never lived to report that the Hatteras light was not lit on the night their ships went down.

Aside from the performance of the lighthouse keepers, within seven years of the lighthouse's construction, in 1810, the station was in need of repair itself. The structure needed attention, and particularly the foundation. The sandy headland upon which Dearborn and his crew erected the lighthouse was slowly blowing away in the constant wind, and erosion threatened to topple the tower. The gravity of the situation was apparent by 1807 when four feet of the stone foundation had been uncovered during the station's first four years of operation. Keepers tried stacking brush around the base of the tower to break the velocity of the wind and to trap the sand. Their efforts yielded acceptable results, but they also set the tone for the next 120 years: the battle with the elements to protect the lighthouse at Cape Hatteras.

Nevertheless, the basic shortcoming of the structure remained the light itself. In 1815 the original lighting apparatus was replaced by a new device patented by Winslow Lewis, a Boston captain who drew from the successful innovations of Swiss inventor Ami Argand to develop a lighting system using improved lamps that were amplified by reflectors. The Argand lamp system was a significant improvement, and Lewis took little time in placing this lighting system in all forty-nine American lighthouses.

Yet despite this improvement, complaints about the Hatteras light multiplied. In 1817, John Delacy of Beaufort wrote to William Crawford, secretary of the treasury, about his dissatisfaction: "The light House at Hatteras particularly is very often without any light in the most tempestuous, and dangerous weather, and it is frequently lighted and kept bright and clear for two and three Hours in the beginning of the night and then permitted to go out entirely which makes it much worse and more dangerous than if there was no light at all shewn."

Captains contended that the lighthouse beacon was too weak to be seen far enough out at sea to do them any good. Before the Revenue Cutter Service had an opportunity to effect changes at Hatteras, a restructuring within the federal government in 1820 shifted the general supervision of the nation's lighthouses from the commissioner of revenue to the office of the fifth auditor of the treasury. The new chief of lighthouse operations was Stephen Pleasonton, a penny-pinching accountant who had little understanding of or appreciation for the role lighthouses and other aids to navigation played in the nation's commerce. For the next thirty years, Pleasonton controlled the fate and the purse strings of the country's lighthouses.

Some small improvements at Cape Hatteras were implemented during Pleasonton's administration, including the acquisition of forty additional acres of land around the base of the lighthouse and the construction of a new keepers quarters in 1827. The ongoing battle to keep the sand from blowing away from the tower's foundation continued relentlessly, however, as did the problem of the limited range of the lighthouse's beacon.

One of the principal challenges with guiding ships around Diamond Shoals was the beacon's inability to penetrate the thick, hazy fog that often hung over the Outer Banks. The dense fog usually hung one hundred above the water, roughly the same elevation as the light on Cape Hatteras's tower.

The fixed white light of Lewis's reflector system was no match for the fog, and lighthouse engineers struggled to find a solution. Some advocated raising the tower. Others, including Pleasonton, suggested lowering it to sixty-five feet so that mariners would be able to see it clearly under the cloud layer.

Pleasonton dispatched Benjamin Isherwood, a chief engineer in the U.S. Navy, to study the problem of the Cape Hatteras Lighthouse. Isherwood was instructed to pay particular attention to the effect of the light on the fog and to decide whether the tower should be raised or lowered. Somewhat predictably, Pleasonton's handpicked inspector supported the chief's conclusions and recommended that the

Fresnel Lens Orders

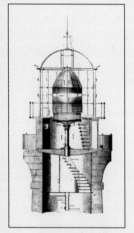
First Order

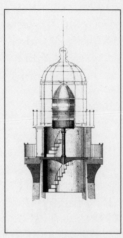
Second Order

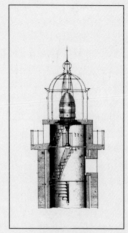
Third Order

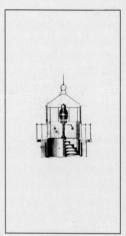
Fourth Order

The Cape Hatteras Light Station has used three first-order Fresnel lenses as well as a second- and a sixth-order lens in the beacon at Cape Point. Orders are based on the size of the lens as measured from the focal point of the lens to the inner lens surface (the radius measurement cited below in millimeters and inches).

Order	Radius (millimeter)	Radius (inches)	Number Built	Number in U.S.	Cost
Hyper-Radial*	1,330	52.3	12	1	$17,000
Meso-Radial*	1,125	44.2	4	0	$14,500
First-Order	920	36.2	467	57	$12,500
Second-Order	700	27.6	261	27	$8,000
Third-Order	500	19.7	384	65	$3,800
Three¹/₂-Order*	375	14.7	12	8	$2,000
Fourth-Order	250	9.8	889	259	$1,250
Fifth-Order	187.5	7.4	580	146	$950
Sixth-Order	150	5.9	635	89	$450
Seventh-Order*	100	4	54	0	$350

*These were modifications of Fresnel's design developed in the late 1880s.

The cited number of Fresnel lenses built in the United States is based on the Findlay Report for 1900. A few more were built in the early 1900s. The actual total may be 5 to 10 percent higher than noted here. Pole lights and lens lanterns are not included.

The cost of each order of lens is based on its reported cost in 1900 and is shown in 1900 dollars.

The Meso-Radial and seventh-order lenses were never used in the United States.

Information courtesy of Thomas Tag

tower should be lowered. In 1851 Pleasonton sought support for this plan. He found little. Moreover, he discovered an increasing number of critics who were calling for an investigation of his administration.

In the eyes of his critics, Pleasonton had done little to improve the overall operation of the Cape Hatteras Lighthouse despite a steady stream of criticism about the quality and dependability of the beacon. As chief of operations, he had approved minor improvements to the Cape Hatteras lantern design in 1834, 1835,

The Hatteras lighthouse was the scene of much innovation as the keepers in residence continually tried to amplify the light. Winslow Lewis paired the original 1782 Argand lamp with a parabolic reflector system to increase the range of the light. Variations of his lighting system, which used a twelve-foot-tall frame and eighteen oil-fed lamps, however, failed to squelch criticisms of the lack of light at Hatteras. Likewise, the job of keeping the oil reservoirs full, cleaning the chimney of each lamp, and polishing the reflectors was a tedious task for the keepers.

With the installation of the Fresnel lens in 1854, however, the sea lanes around Cape Hatteras became safer. When this lens was combined with an incandescent oil vapor lamp (IOV) around 1913, the range of the light was increased significantly. This combination remained in operation until 1935 when erosion threatened to topple the tower and the Bureau of Lighthouses closed the light station. It was replaced by an electric light atop a 150-foot skeletal steel tower.

In the late 1930s and early 1940s vandals and souvenir hunters removed the prisms from the Fresnel mechanism in the unmanned brick tower. Other parts of the lens were stolen when the apparatus was stored in the Little Kinnakeet Lifesaving Station. Recently, people have "found" some of the missing prisms in attics or on display in homes and have returned them to the National Park Service, facilitating to some degree the restoration of the magnificent 1870 first-order Fresnel lens.

The park service now maintains the lighthouse as part of Cape Hatteras National Seashore. To recreate the working historic district of the early twentieth century, the park service has requested a first-order Fresnel lens from the Coast Guard, reasoning that the Fresnel device was more representative of the period in which the lighthouse was in operation than the present optic, a digitally controlled beacon with two twenty-four-inch drum lights.

The incandescent oil vapor (IOV) lamp (left) was a big step toward increasing the brightness of the Hatteras light. Vaporized kerosene burned with a brighter light than the original eighteen-lamp array. This IOV lamp and oil reservoir (right) replaced the original oil lamp and increased the candle power from 27,000 to 80,000, making the Hatteras lighthouse the brightest navigational aid on the East Coast.

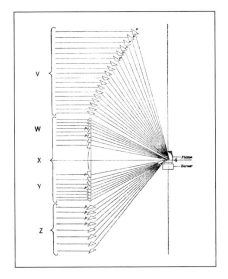

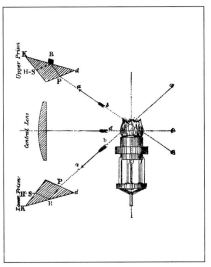

Augustin Fresnel's lens captured 90 percent of its light source and magnified it through a prism array to generate and project a beam as far as nineteen miles out to sea. The first diagram to the far left illustrates the positioning of Fresnel's prisms to create the parallel elements of such a strong light. The detail in the illustration to the near left demonstrates how light is refracted by the prisms before it is reflected outward. These diagrams first appeared in the 1886 publication *All Among the Lighthouses* by Mary B. Crowninshield.

1837, 1840, 1845, and 1847, but each modification continued to employ the Argand lamp and reflector system touted by Lewis, who also happened to be Pleasonton's good friend. Most damning, however, was the fact that the series of modifications made to the tower's lamp had consistently ignored the technological advances in lighting that were being introduced in Europe.

By 1850 the tide of public opinion had turned against Pleasonton. His continued insistence on the use of reflector-lamp technology had allowed the United States to slip embarrassingly behind in the international quest for reliable navigational aids. Lighthouses throughout Europe employed the relatively new Fresnel lens, a beautiful beehive of light collected from a central source and projected in brilliant flashes that could be seen many more miles out to sea than their fixed-light reflective counterparts.

American captains sailing overseas had seen the new technology in use. Moreover, they were amazed and angered that Pleasonton had refused to purchase the new Fresnel system. When he would not listen to their pleas for improved navigational lights, they turned to their elected officials. It was Pleasonton's undoing.

In March 1851, Congress established a review board to assess the American lighthouse establishment and to recommend areas for expansion and improvements. This group, composed of two high-ranking naval officers, two Army Corps of Engineers officers, and the superintendent of the U.S. Coast Survey, traveled domestically and abroad, gathering information, interviewing captains and scientists, and inspecting various lighthouses.

It did not take long for the Lighthouse Review Board to note the criticisms about the light at Cape Hatteras. Captains from military

Following improvements in 1854, the lighthouse displayed a new first-order Fresnel lens atop a 150-foot tower. The exterior was painted red and white to increase visibility during the day.

and commercial ships were more than willing to share their experiences with the Cape Hatteras Lighthouse. "[The Hatteras Light is] the most important on our coast, and without a doubt, the worst light in the world. . . . The first nine trips I made I never saw Hatteras light at all, though frequently passing in sight of the breakers; and when I did see, I could not tell it from a steamer's light, excepting that the steamer's lights are much brighter," reported one captain. "Cape Hatteras and the Tortugas lights are a disgrace to the country. . . . The lights on Hatteras, Lookout, Canaveral, and Cape Florida, if not improved, had better be dispensed with, as the navigator is apt to run ashore looking for them."

In 1852 the review board submitted a 750-page report to the secretary of the treasury outlining the deficiencies throughout the U.S. lighthouse establishment and recommending significant technological and operational improvements. At the top of their list of concerns was the condition and effectiveness of the Cape Hatteras Lighthouse. In their congressional report, they outlined the light's importance and the need for several improvements.

There is perhaps no light on the entire coast of the United States of greater value to the commerce and navigation of the country than this. That it is not such a light as any sea-coast light should be, is too apparent to require much argument; while its special requirements, having reference to the Gulf-stream, the currents and counter-currents which sweep past it, and the very dangerous shoals, extending to a distance of ten nautical miles from the light, all tend to make it of no ordinary importance. Vessels, propelled both by wind and steam, run for soundings off this cape; and it is of first importance to navigators wishing to make quick passages, that they should use this light going south. At present it is of very little use, in consequence of its limited range. Navigators do not, as a general rule, rely upon it sufficiently to warrant them in running for it. It is fitted with fifteen lamps and twenty one inch reflectors, having an elevation of about ninety-five feet, which would give a range, under favorable circumstances, of fourteen and a half nautical miles, provided the apparatus for illuminating was of the best description.

There is no single light on the coast believed to require renovation more than this does. An elevation of one hundred and fifty feet, and a first-class illuminating apparatus, are imperiously demanded and without any unnecessary delay.

20

The thorough and objective work of the Lighthouse Review Board prompted Congress to authorize the creation of a new body—the Light-House Board—which was to operate directly under the secretary of the treasury and oversee the country's lighthouses. Composed mostly of members of the original review board, in October 1852 the new board immediately addressed the problems at Cape Hatteras.

The Light-House Board asked the Corps of Engineers to determine how best to raise the lighthouse tower and ordered the installation of a first-order Fresnel lens and lantern. After an initial field study supported the idea, the board obtained a $15,000 appropriation for the necessary improvements. The funding covered the costs of raising the tower to a height of 150 feet, outfitting the beacon with a Fresnel lens and lantern, and constructing a new double keepers quarters at the light station.

In 1854 the improvements began. Masons erected a five-story brick addition at the top of Dearborn's fifty-year-old sandstone tower. Lampists installed the new rotating Fresnel lens, and the beacon was soon visible twenty miles at sea. To improve the lighthouse's visibility to sailors, the tower exterior was painted in two colors. The bottom seventy feet of the tower were painted white, to allow the light to stand out against the green woods of Hatteras Island, and the upper eighty feet were painted red, to make the tower stand out against the blue Carolina sky.

The original 1854 first-order Fresnel lens installed at Cape Hatteras was manufactured in St. Gobin, France. Its prisms were "crown-glass," tinted green from iron oxide content and individually handcrafted. The lens itself was formed by installing hundreds of prisms in bronze frames held together with lead and

To figure the limits of visibility of a Fresnel lens, take the square root of the height of the lighthouse at its focal plane and multiply that by 1.15 (considered the mariner's constant; a nautical mile equals 1.15 statute miles). Add to the answer the square root of 15 (3.87) times 1.15 (the average mariner is 15 feet above sea level). The sum is the limit of visibility of the Fresnel lens from the lighthouse being considered.

For example, the height of a lighthouse at the focal plane is 150 feet. The square root of 150 is 12.25, multiplied by 1.15 equals 14.09. The square root of 15 is 3.87, multiplied by 1.15 equals 4.45. Add the two products together: 14.09+4.45=18.54. Rounded to 19 nautical miles, this should be the distance given for the range of a first-order Fresnel lens, the typical lens in a lighthouse 150 or more feet tall.

If a mariner is closer to sea level, the limits of visibility will be lower, and if the sailor is on a larger ship at a greater height above the water, the limits of visibility will be greater.

Source: *Mariner's Notebook* by Capt. William P. Crawford, Master Mariner

linseed oil (called Lafarge). The finished lens was crated and shipped to the lighthouse depot on Staten Island, New York, and then to Hatteras Island.

Keeper William O'Neal and a lampist assembled the bronze frames at the top of the Cape Hatteras Lighthouse. The optic, also called a lenticular system, involved a revolving lens that produced six brilliant beams of light per minute. The light that poured over Hatteras Island that first night in 1854 after the installation of the new lens was more intense than any that had shone before.

During the next decade the modified Dearborn tower held three of these optical wonders: a revolving first-order Fresnel lens in 1854, a second-order Fresnel lens in 1862 when Hatteras was occupied by Federal troops, and another first-order lens in 1863. Indicative of the significance of the Cape Hatteras Lighthouse, the Lighthouse Service approved installation of a first-order Fresnel lens when a new lighthouse was constructed at Cape Hatteras in 1870.

All of the 1854 improvements succeeded in enhancing the light station's mission. The brighter light shining from a higher altitude meant that ships could finally see the lighthouse from safe water as they rounded Cape Hatteras. For the next few years the Hatteras light enjoyed a respite from the previous half-century of criticism. By the late 1850s, the Hatteras lighthouse was one of the nation's premier light stations, towering 150 feet above the island and emitting its powerful flash across the shifting shoals to the east.

Problems, however, were again on the horizon as war clouds gathered over the country. By 1860 the future was all too clear. The next few years would be a time of darkness, especially for the lighthouses of North Carolina.

3

THE CIVIL WAR

SENTINELS IN GRAY AND BLUE

We will demolish the light at Hatteras if we do no more.
CONFEDERATE COL. A. R. WRIGHT

WHEN WAR BROKE OUT between the states in 1861, the achievements the Light-House Board had worked so hard to accomplish were quickly undone. Prior to the war, North Carolina's coastal lights had been equipped with Fresnel lenses and the inlets and channels were well marked with light vessels, screw-pile lights, and buoys. The treacherous waters of the Outer Banks were finally safer for ships. During the earliest days of the war, however, the dangerous nature of the Carolina coast that had prompted the implementation of these navigational aids thrust the region into the forefront of the war planners. Both sides recognized the strategic value of the barrier islands and their inlets and the broad sounds and headwaters of the area's primary rivers. Whoever controlled these inlets and sounds would dominate a significant portion of the eastern coastland.

Along the northern Outer Banks, Hatteras Inlet had become the primary point of passage to the sea. Deeper and more dependable than Ocracoke Inlet, the fifteen-year-old inlet at Hatteras, which opened during the same 1846 storm that had created Oregon Inlet, became the focus of attention for both sides.

In 1861 Union troops camped around the Hatteras lighthouse. This sketch appeared in *Harper's Weekly* and is one of the rare views of the 1803 tower. At the outbreak of the war, Confederates removed the first-order Fresnel lens and shipped it to the mainland for safekeeping (at least one report claimed that it was destroyed). The Southerners used the lantern room for a lookout post, but Union forces put an end to that in August 1861, when the Federals captured Hatteras Inlet and the lighthouse. The following year a second-order Fresnel lens was installed, and in 1863 a new revolving first-order lens replaced that. The light remained active for the remainder of the war.

This illustration shows the Twentieth Indiana Regiment camped at the base of the tower following the first day of the so-called Chicamacomico Races in late 1861. The following morning, Union troops counterattacked, forcing the Confederates north along Hatteras Island and saving the lighthouse.

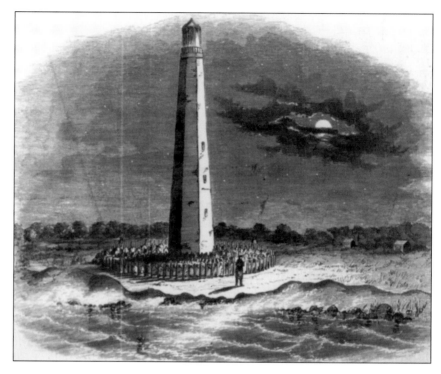

After North Carolina seceded from the Union on May 20, 1861, state troops moved to the Outer Banks and took control of the lighthouses and the other navigational aids. Shortly after the outbreak of hostilities in mid-April, President Abraham Lincoln ordered a blockade of Southern commerce, focusing particular importance on the inlets of the Outer Banks. Meanwhile, North Carolina troops wasted no time in extinguishing the beacons that might aid Union shipping in the offshore sea-lanes. Southerners had little need for the lights themselves, since their ships now needed to run an armored gauntlet to escape their own ports.

Northerners were incensed by the elimination of the lights. "Soon after the bombardment of Fort Sumter, the Confederate Government, with that murderous indifference to human life which has distinguished them from the first, extinguished all the lights they could reach, and among others the lighthouse erected at Cape Hatteras," wrote one Federal sailor.

The elimination of the lighthouse beacons was only the beginning. North Carolina officials had already moved to take advantage of the natural defenses their state's shoreline provided. The shallow inlets and shoal-marked sounds provided perfect hiding places for blockade-runners and privateers. Even before the state left the Union, plans were being put in place for the protection of the North Carolina coast.

"The Governor of North Carolina had, before the state regularly joined the Confederacy, been going it on his own hook, as it were," remembered Confederate Capt. William Parker in his memoirs. "He fitted out privateers, sent out blockade-runners, etc., and got in so many stores, that it was observed at the beginning of the war that the North Carolina troops were the best armed and best clothed men that passed through Richmond. The steamer *Winslow,* a small side-wheeled boat under Captain Thomas M. Crossan, formerly of the Navy, was very active in cruising outside Cape Hatteras as a privateer, and captured some valuable prizes."

The small fleet of lightly armed vessels that patrolled North Carolina's waters so annoyed Union interests that it became known as the "Mosquito Fleet." Like the winged creatures for which they were named, the Confederate craft were easily destroyed if caught, but they possessed a distinct advantage over their opponents in terms of speed and quickness. Flitting about the coast, striking unsuspecting ships, and retreating when threatened by larger and more powerful Northern warships, the tiny vessels were effective. One ship, the *Winslow,* which was referred to above, captured sixteen Federal ships off Hatteras Island during a six-week period.

On shore the Confederates set up sentry posts in the lighthouses along the Outer Banks. They also constructed a series of forts to protect against an assault from the sea. Two forts—Clark and Hatteras—were built at Hatteras Inlet. Safe behind these fortifications, the Southern captains operated with relative impunity.

At the center of these Confederate fortifications, standing high above the sand, sound, and sea, was the Cape Hatteras Lighthouse. With its light extinguished and its Fresnel lens removed and shipped to the mainland for safekeeping, the tower was transformed into a lookout post. The federal government had labored so hard to build this spire and so long to make it an effective navigational aid, and ironically it was now being used against it.

In August 1861, Union Lt. Thomas Selfridge informed Gideon Welles, the secretary of the navy, of the military situation at Hatteras Inlet:

> It seems that the coast of Carolina is infested with a nest of privateers that have thus far escaped capture, and, in the ingenious method of their cruising, are probably likely to avoid the clutches of our cruisers. Hatteras Inlet, a little south of Cape Hatteras light, seems their principal rendezvous. Here they have a fortification that protects them from assault. A lookout in the light-house proclaims the coast clear, and a merchantman in sight; they dash out and are

back again in a day with their prize. So long as these remain it will be impossible to entirely prevent their depredations, for they do not venture out when men-of-war are in sight; and, in the bad weather of the coming season, cruisers can not always keep their stations off these inlets with great risk of going ashore.

Welles wasted no time in directing his commander of the Atlantic Blockading Squadron, Adm. Silas Stringham, to concentrate his efforts on the Carolina coast: "There is no position off the coast which you are guarding that requires greater vigilance or where the well-directed efforts and demonstrations would be more highly appreciated by the government and country than North Carolina, which has been the resort of pirates and their abettors."

Stringham's response came in the form of a seven-ship flotilla with twenty-five hundred soldiers and sailors. Outnumbering the Confederates by nearly three to one, the ships arrived off Hatteras Inlet on the afternoon of August 27, 1861. The following morning, in the first combined effort using naval bombardment and amphibious assault in U.S. history, the Union attacked.

The confrontation proved to be a lopsided affair. Using newly developed rifled naval guns, the Federal gunners easily outpaced their Southern counterparts, raining artillery fire into the forts at a rate of thirty shells per minute while Confederate lead plopped short of their targets and fell harmlessly into Pamlico Sound.

It took less than two days for the forts to capitulate. Despite the furious bombardment, Southern casualties were light, with seven killed and approximately forty wounded. Northern troops were unscathed, with no reports of fatalities or injuries. The Union commanders were elated, as were their superiors in Washington, because the successful action came on the heels of the depressing and demoralizing Federal defeat at the battle of First Manassas. "This was our first naval victory—indeed our first victory of any kind, and great was the rejoicing throughout the United States," recalled Union Adm. David Porter.

Once Federal troops took control of Hatteras Inlet and the area around the Cape Hatteras Lighthouse, they immediately began the work of relighting the beacon. Although the Confederates had removed the valuable Fresnel lens, the rest of the lighting apparatus and the tower itself were intact and unharmed. Still, the loss of the lens presented problems for the Union engineers who had to remove portions of the remaining lantern room machinery prior to installing a new light. Before that work could begin, however, the battle for Hatteras Island and the Cape Hatteras Lighthouse was rejoined.

Many Outer Banks residents found themselves in an awkward situation when the Civil War began. Although they were residents of North Carolina, most had much more in common with their Northern cousins than with their Southern brothers. Captains and sailors had frequented northern ports before the war and had made significant investments of time and money in friendships and business dealings there. They had been more likely to visit New York than Raleigh, which must have seemed a world away across the broad, boggy mainland plain of North Carolina.

As a result, not all Outer Banks residents were elated when the state seceded from the Union on May 20, 1861, and a significant portion of the local population welcomed the victorious Northern troops following the battle of Hatteras Inlet in August 1861. In a report to his superiors, Col. Rush Hawkins, commander of the Ninth New York, a flamboyant Zouave regiment, recorded the plight of the local residents in the captured territory on Hatteras Island: "The people on this strip of land have been peculiarly situated. Since the secession of this state, their means of subsistence have been completely taken away and now they are mostly without food or clothing."

Shortly after the battle for Hatteras, about 250 islanders offered to take an oath of allegiance to the United States, which Hawkins administered. He later reported administering the oath to additional groups in the eastern part of the state. In fact, Hawkins added, a group was already working to create a new provisional government in eastern North Carolina, something the Union should support with force if necessary. "Could this be done now . . . one third of North Carolina would be back in the Union within two weeks," he said in September 1861.

Good relations between the islanders and Union troops were strained after some of the soldiers vandalized homes and plundered livestock and gardens to augment their monotonous military rations. Hawkins was furious and did the best he could to control his troops, but some islanders had had enough of soldiers from both sides.

Despite the behavior of some of the garrisoned troops on Hatteras, the counter-Secessionist movement continued to move forward. Two men—Marble Nash Taylor, a Virginia-born Methodist minister, and Charles Henry Foster, a Maine native who had run a newspaper on the North Carolina mainland—traveled to New York City to generate support and financial backing for the new provisional government and the relief of its citizens.

Finding support in respectable quarters, the pair returned to the Outer Banks and began organizing a meeting that became known as the Hatteras Convention. On November 18, 1861, supporters gathered in Hatteras Village, where they issued a proclamation urging the repeal of secession and a return to the Union. They elected Taylor provisional governor and Foster as their congressional representative. Not long after the convention, Foster traveled to Washington, D.C., to take the seat in Congress he was "rightfully if not legally" entitled to. An unimpressed and disinterested House rebuffed him.

History has not been kind to the memory of Taylor and Foster. Both were accused at the time of pursuing personal gain rather than the common good. They were understandably unpopular amongst Southern loyalists. A news correspondent for the *Fayetteville Observer* painted a vitriolic picture of Taylor a month after the Hatteras Convention: "Marble Taylor is emphatically a small man—small in stature, small in mind, small in morals. His tallow complexion resembles a whited sepulchre, and his eyes, mouth, and chin resemble dead men's bones."

The refusal of Congress to recognize Foster doomed the counter-Secessionist movement, and as news of the Hatteras Convention spread, its supporters were roundly criticized and its leaders arrested. As one Southern newspaper put it at the time, Taylor and Foster's paper government "collapsed in the faces of those who were conjuring up illusions for the delusion of others."

A month after the capture of the Hatteras Inlet forts, Union commanders began to move against the considerable Confederate fortifications on Roanoke Island, approximately forty miles north at the northern end of Pamlico Sound. Six hundred troops from the Twentieth Indiana Regiment were sent to the northern Hatteras Island village of Chicamacomico (now Rodanthe) to establish a base and defend it against attack.

The Indianans were to be supplied by a tugboat, but the tugboat and its crew were captured by elements of the Mosquito Fleet. During the questioning of the crew, one of the prisoners told an exaggerated tale of there being two thousand Union troops at Chicamacomico who were poised to attack Roanoke Island.

Assuming that the best defense is a good offense, the Confederate commander on Roanoke Island dispatched the Third Georgia Infantry to attack the Federals from the north while North Carolina troops attacked from the south. After defeating the Union force at Chicamacomico, the combined Confederates were then to proceed south with the objective of destroying the Cape Hatteras Lighthouse. "We will demolish the light at Hatteras if we do no more," boasted Col. A. R. Wright, commander of the Third Georgia.

The Union commander at Chicamacomico saw the two-pronged attack looming across the sound and quickly ordered his troops south to Buxton and the Hatteras light before the North Carolina troops could land and cut them off. The Federal troops, along with many of the residents of the northern Hatteras Island villages, ran for their lives, convinced a mighty Confederate fighting force was approaching.

For the soldiers—Northerners and Southerners alike—who were stationed on the Outer Banks, the islands were an amazingly inhospitable place. The same conditions would be endured by the construction crews who built the Cape Hatteras Lighthouses. Edward Warren, a Confederate doctor stationed at Hatteras Inlet in 1861, wrote:

The human mind can scarcely conceive of the loneliness and desolation of the place. Imagine, if you can, a narrow strip of land interposed between two great wastes of water—one half consisting of a bog with a few stunted trees and shrubs scattered over its surface and peopled with innumerable frogs and snakes, and the remainder composed of sand so unpalatable as to be lifted in clouds of dust by every passing breeze, and you will have some idea of the topography of that God-forsaken place.

The mosquitoes held possession of it by day and night, blackening the air with their presence, and making it vocal with their eternal hum. A sable cloud composed of myriads of these insects, and visible for a considerable distance, hovered over the head of every living thing that stood or walked upon that dreary shore, and while one laborer worked upon the fortifications another had to stand by him with a handful of brush to keep him from being devoured by them. The poor mules look as if they had been drawn through key-holes and then attacked with eruptions of small pox.

The Northerners reached the Hatteras light at nightfall and were reinforced by troops from the Ninth New York. The Confederates camped a few miles north of the lighthouse. Both sides prepared to fight the next morning. The Confederate plan, however, encountered a serious problem. The ships carrying the North Carolina troops had run aground more than two miles from shore, south of Chicamacomico. A quick head count on both sides at dawn the next day showed the Georgians, lacking their reinforcements, were well outnumbered. Now it was the Union's turn to play the role of pursuer.

Federal troops advanced to the north across the same sand they had retreated over the previous afternoon. The strange running battle came to be known as the "Chicamacomico Races." Little in the way of tactical advantage was gained by either side, but the Cape Hatteras Lighthouse survived. The Bodie Island Lighthouse was not as fortunate. Confederate engineers demolished it before the Southerners' final retreat to Roanoke Island.

With the Confederates expelled from the island, ship captains again pushed for the relighting of the Hatteras beacon. In March 1862 the Light-House Board ordered district engineer W. J. Newman to assess what was needed to put the Cape Hatteras Lighthouse back into commission. Newman traveled to the site and found the tower and most of the beacon apparatus still intact. Although it would take some time to prepare the lantern for relighting, he determined that the task was not insurmountable.

A far bigger problem, Newman reported, was the state of the lighthouse itself. Cracks were appearing in the sandstone portion of the tower, and the brick portion needed painting. Winds had eroded and scoured the base of the tower, and Newman recommended paving the area around the base with tar if officials wanted to preserve the lighthouse. In addition, the tower stairs were wood and "most inconvenient, the windows defective, etc." Newman speculated that it might be cheaper to start all over.

In one of his reports, the district engineer addressed the continued risk to the lighthouse and its keepers, despite the fact that Union troops had pushed the Confederate forces far from the Outer Banks. Fearing the lighthouse might be attacked by Southern partisans once the light was restored, Newman requested a detachment of troops to guard the lighthouse. He cited as his primary concern the well-being of the keeper: "The [Lighthouse] Tower is removed some distance from the Dwelling. The stairway to the summit is nothing more than a series of heavy wooden ladders and landings, made of yellow pine and most inflammable. At the base of the Tower a large quantity of dry brush is always placed to keep sand from blowing away. Any evil disposed person could in a few minutes, landing in the woods on the Sound Side, collect the dry stuff, fire the Stairway, and the man on watch at the top of the Tower would not have a chance to escape."

To refurbish the Hatteras light, Newman recommended a second-order Fresnel lens. The request was approved and took awhile to fill, but by early June 1862 the light was again operational. The following year a first-order Fresnel lens, "combining the latest and highest improvements," was ordered and installed at the Cape Hatteras Light Station. The lighthouse was now back in the same condition it had been prior to the war, with a first-order Fresnel lens marking Diamond Shoals at night and the red-and-white tower warning of the danger by day.

The state of the tower, however, could not be ignored. What a war had failed to accomplish, nature was completing one grain of sand at a time. The headland upon which the tower had been built was gone, leaving the lighthouse in a perilous predicament. Newman's hunch that a new lighthouse at Hatteras might be the best course of action soon proved correct.

The Cape Hatteras Lighthouse on North Carolina's Outer Banks is at the bend of the "elbow" of Hatteras Island. It lies one mile north of Cape Point, along the barrier islands where the coastline turns sharply to the west, and separated from the mainland by the Pamlico Sound. Because Cape Hatteras protrudes significantly into the Atlantic, many mariners who attempted to round this notorious spot became victims of the dangerous shoals and unpredictable weather off this point.

Below, an artist has represented the two main lighthouses that have stood at Hatteras. The two illustrations to the left depict the 1803 Dearborn tower as it was constructed originally and following enhancements in 1854. The two images on the right show the 1870 Stetson tower as it looked shortly after its completion, with a red brick superstructure, and since 1873, when the lighthouse received its familiar black-and-white spirals as a prominent day mark.

CAPE HATTERAS

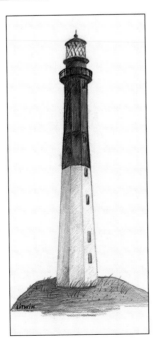
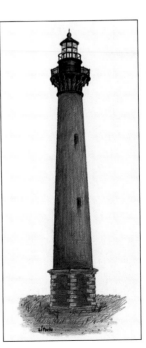

The Cape Hatteras Lighthouse marks the edge of America. In consideration of its history, architectural detail, and contribution to the nation as an icon of lighthouses, it has joined the honored ranks of Historic National Landmarks.

Right: For more than a century the keepers at Hatteras would extinguish the flame of the oil lamp at this moment, draw the linen curtains to block the harsh sun, and prepare the lantern for the next evening's work as the Guardian of the Graveyard of the Atlantic.

The most treacherous area of the shipping lanes around Cape Hatteras is a region of shallow underwater sandy hills known as Diamond Shoals. Because there was no way to build an adequate foundation for a lighthouse on these shoals, the only option for a navigable light was to anchor a lightship on the position. As is apparent in this illustration from *Harper's Weekly,* the waters could be harrowingly rough, pitching the vessel violently in all directions and making the duty hazardous for everyone aboard. In general, these crews described their stints as a sort of imprisonment punctuated by seasickness and boredom. This image is from the 1850s. The vessel has only one sail, and the smoke from the burning lamp suggests the fuel for the light is whale oil. Most of these early lightships were awkward in the water, designed to remain anchored in one place rather than travel. Until the late nineteenth century, these vessels were towed into position and tethered to the bottom with tons of chain and anchors. Crews often complained that these ships could not "sail before the wind," leaving the craft and its crew at the mercy of the elements. Understandably, there was a high turnover for the months-long duty aboard the Hatteras lightships.

Left: At dusk a solitary figure on the beach enjoys a private show as a photoelectric cell illuminates the Cape Hatteras lighthouse beacon for its night's work.

The Bodie Island Light Station, above, is also in the Cape Hatteras National Seashore. This lighthouse is one of the classic tall coastal lights designed after the prototype at Cape Lookout, North Carolina. Its beauty is highlighted in this photograph by a rare snowstorm in early 1995.

Other Outer Banks lighthouses include, top left, Currituck Beach (built in 1875), top right, Ocracoke (1823), and lower left, Cape Lookout (1859). Currituck Beach and Cape Lookout are tall coastal lights marking points along the shore for seagoing ships. The shorter Ocracoke serves as a harbor light for local coasting vessels.

This first-order Fresnel lens (right) was removed from the 1870 Hatteras tower and transferred to the Pigeon Point Lighthouse (below) in California in 1872. It has twenty-four panels housing a total of 1,008 prisms. The Fresnel lens that replaced this one at Hatteras upon completion of the Stetson tower in 1870 subsequently was vandalized during a time when the lighthouse was left open and unsupervised. Only pieces of it remain on exhibit at Cape Hatteras and Bodie Island to remind visitors of its original splendor.

Right: The imposing size of the Cape Hatteras Lighthouse is not apparent until the couple to the right is brought into comparison.

The 1854 double keepers quarters (right) and the 1872 principal keepers quarters (below) are pictured here several months before being moved to the new site as part of the relocation of the light station. When the move is completed, all of the buildings will be positioned as they were at the original site so that visitors will see the station as it was during the late nineteenth century in its original relation to the sea.

Facing page: Modern details contrast with older elements in these images. The dual aerobeacon (top) provided the beacon when the tower was relighted in 1950 after it became part of the Cape Hatteras National Seashore. The granite accents (lower left), including the corner stones or quoins, accentuate the base of the tower. The iron brackets that support the lantern room (bottom right) were fashioned by Bartlett and Robbins, a well-known Baltimore foundry that did most of the ironwork for the lighthouse.

The aerial view of Hatteras above (left), looking south, was taken in the mid-1960s. The path from the 1870 tower to the ruins of the 1803 tower is still visible. That section of the beach, however, is missing in the photograph on the right, which was taken in 1998 and reveals the development surrounding the lighthouse along the narrow barrier island to the north. In the latter photograph, the closeness of the sea to the base of the lighthouse is dramatically apparent.

Facing page: Counterclockwise from the lower left, a brief tour of the Cape Hatteras lighthouse includes the black-and-white marble floor at the entryway. Next is a photograph of the iron handrail and one of the stair landings among the 264 steps to the top, which is illuminated by the natural light of a window. A south-facing window gives a view of the breakers below, and finally, top left, visitors take in the panoramic view of Hatteras Island from the catwalk.

The double keepers quarters (above) begins its relocation journey while National Park Service personnel, media, and lighthouse volunteers look on. At the lighthouse (below), Joe Jakubik, the project manager of the relocation, stands on the original pine-timber mat and points to the bottom of plinth number two, protected by steel beams. Plinth number one will be removed and reset after the lighthouse has been moved.

Right: At the edge of the sea, workers begin the excavation and dewatering of the foundation in preparation for the relocation of the lighthouse.

The move corridor can be clearly seen in the photograph to the right. The double keepers quarters and brick oil house wait at the end of the path where they will be joined by the principal keepers quarters and the lighthouse. Below is an artist's conception of how the lighthouse will appear in the "ready to roll" stage of the move process. Oak cribbing and steel beams will be used to lift the lighthouse onto a path of roll beams, the tracks along which the lighthouse will slide to its new foundation. The push jacks seen in the lower left, will gently propel the tower at an indiscernable rate, twenty-nine hundred feet to the southwest over a four- to six-week period.

PART 2

THE STETSON TOWER

4

THE SECOND
LIGHTHOUSE

A NEW ERA IN BRICK

When completed it will be the most imposing and substantial
brick lighthouse on this continent, if not the world.
LIGHT-HOUSE BOARD ANNUAL REPORT, 1869

As THE LIGHT-HOUSE BOARD worked to repair and restore Dearborn's 1803 lighthouse, district engineer W. J. Newman saw a much different solution to more than six decades of problems with the lighthouse at Cape Hatteras. In 1867, when the Light-House Board requested funds to repair the aging wooden stairs in the tower, Newman estimated that repairs to the lighthouse could cost as much or more than construction of a new one. When the board members received a bid of $20,000 to replace the tower's interior wooden staircase with one made of iron, they began to think Newman might be right.

Newman also pointed to other problems plaguing the light, not the least of which was the nearly constant battle to keep sand around the tower's foundation. The unstable foundation made the tower weak and susceptible to the effects of the violent weather that often battered the Outer Banks. "The vibrations during heavy gales are alarming and the cracks in the old Tower are extending," Newman reported. "The structure is quite out of date, and liable sooner or later to be a disaster."

Newman's argument proved to be persuasive. In March 1867 Congress appropriated $75,000 for the construction of a new lighthouse for Cape Hatteras. This was not to be just any lighthouse, however; it was to be built to the highest standards. After sixty years, lighthouse officials wanted a light at Hatteras that they could depend upon. The board concluded, "In a tower so expensive and exposed as the new one proposed for Cape Hatteras will be, it is desirable to take every measure to secure the very best materials . . . quality is a much greater object than price."

When the first set of blueprints for the second Cape Hatteras Lighthouse were prepared, the planners assumed the height of the focal plane of the tower would be 150 feet, similar to the 1859 Cape Lookout Lighthouse design from which the Hatteras plans were adapted. Merchants and mariners, however, clamored for more. In the end, their efforts to increase the height of the Hatteras tower were successful.

"Since the estimate for this work has been submitted to Congress it has been found that the interests of commerce require a tower of much greater elevation than was provided for," reported the Light-House Board in 1868. "At the time of making the estimate it was supposed that a tower of 150 feet in height (the ordinary altitude of first order towers) would answer every requirement, but it is now deemed necessary to erect a structure having a focal plane of 180 feet. This increased height will augment the cost of the structure, and an estimate of the additional amount required ($40,000) is submitted."

The new structure eventually became the crown jewel of North Carolina lighthouses. Towering over everything else within one hundred miles, the new lighthouse was the first in a series of three lights the Light-House Board would build from Cape Hatteras to the Virginia border between 1869 and 1875. Placed at forty-mile intervals, Bodie Island and Currituck Beach Lighthouses soon joined the Hatteras light as the country's newest coastal towers. The placement of the trio ensured that ship captains would always have one of the beacons in sight as they cruised the coast; as one light fell away off their stern, another would come into view off their bow.

The Light-House Board approached the construction of the new tower with the lessons learned from the old one clearly in mind. According to their 1869 annual report:

> The site selected bear north by east 600 feet distant from the old tower, and therefore as near it as well could be. The sailing directions will be very slightly affected if at all. It is on the general level of the beach, and therefore secure from the destructive action of the wind, which has always so seriously threatened the foundations of the old

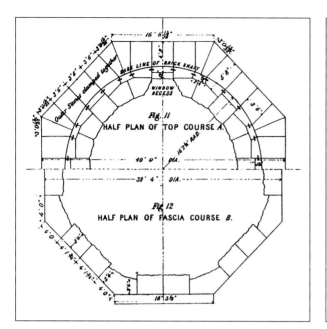

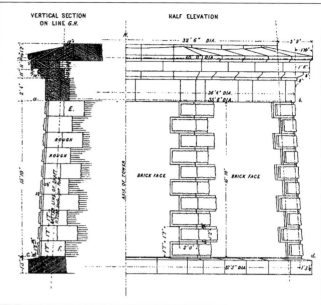

tower, and to counteract which very heavy expense was incurred through many years. The site is also above the highest level of the sea and so far removed from the water line as to render it safe from encroachment from the sea.

The tower itself will consist of a frustum on a right cone of 150 feet in perpendicular height, resting on an octagonal base of 24 feet in height, and 45½ feet in diameter at the lowest plinth course. The foundation is rubble granite; the plinth courses, quoins, and cornice, of cut granite, and the rest of the structure of brick and iron. The whole will be surmounted of a lens of the first order, a focal plane of which will be 180 feet above the ground and 184 feet above the sea. When completed it will be the most imposing and substantial brick lighthouse on this continent, if not the world.

Architectural details from the Lighthouse Board's plans for the 1870 Cape Hatteras tower exhibit the depth in planning for the impressive base. The eight-sided lower portion was designed in keeping with the architectural style of the 1803 tower. The distinguished granite quoins, or corner stones, of the eight-sided brick base further embellished the design.

The board took a much different approach from the micromanagement techniques employed by Pleasonton. Construction supervisors were allowed to perform most of the on-site management and decision-making and to contract for whatever goods and services an individual project might require. District engineers supervised the entire operation and often performed field inspections of work while it was in progress. The construction supervisor for the Cape Hatteras Lighthouse project was Dexter Stetson, an ingenious man who proved to be perfect for the job.

In November 1868 Stetson arrived on Hatteras Island with a working party to begin preliminary preparations for the construction project. Like Dearborn before him, Stetson first had to provide

In his 1893 documentation of the Cape Hatteras Light Station, Lighthouse Service surveyor and photographer H. Bamber included these drawings of the site. He showed both the 1803 and 1870 tower locations along with their associated buildings and their positions in relation to the ocean. Bamber noted on his sketch that the first floor of the tower was 15.73 feet "above water level." The remnants of the sand hill upon which the first tower was built can be seen ringing the remains of the foundation in the illustration to the right. The site plan below shows the 1870 tower and the two keepers houses and their outbuildings. Each quarters had a separate detached kitchen, storehouse, and privy. Fences around the houses and the lighthouse kept grazing livestock at bay. The facing page shows an elevation drawing of the Stetson tower.

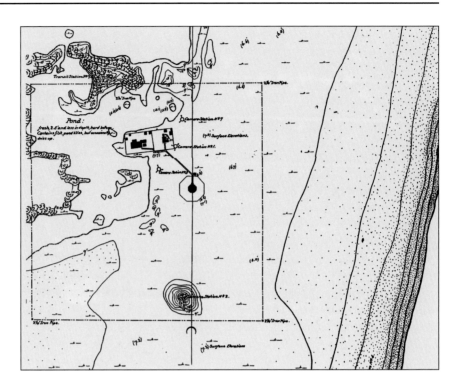

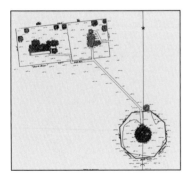

accommodations for his crew. Unlike Dearborn, who found little in the way of available housing on the island in 1800, Stetson was able to rent a house on the beach until his workers could begin their own quarters.

In less than a month, Stetson's men had built a barracks and mess room, a blacksmith shop, two derricks, and a storage building for cement and other perishable items near the site for the new tower. A mile and a quarter away on the shores of Pamlico Sound they built three lightering boats, a smaller boat, a crane, and a substantial wharf. Connecting the two work sites was a tram railroad that negotiated the same boggy undergrowth that Dearborn's men and oxen had contended with.

Before long, the first of the 1¼ million dark red bricks and dressed granite blocks began to arrive at the site. The bricks came from kilns along the James River, and the granite was chopped from a Vermont quarry not far from the New Hampshire quarry that had provided the sandstone for the original tower. Each load had to be transferred from larger ships to the lighters and unloaded onto the wharf, placed on the tram railway, and hauled to the construction site. It was a laborious process made none the easier by the exposed nature of the soundside landing. Accidents occurred, including the loss of a key shipment of granite in five feet of water within sight of the wharf.

There were also losses at sea. One ship carrying 100,000 bricks for the lighthouse sank in a gale near the cape, and another carrying 50,000 bricks sank off Nags Head. The losses created work delays that were exacerbated by the substandard performance of Lennox and Burgess, the firm the Light-House Board had contracted to provide transportation for the lighthouse project.

Lennox and Burgess had apparently neglected to tell the board that it had no ships available for transport when it entered into the agreement. This oversight became painfully clear to all involved when the November 15, 1868, deadline for the delivery of materials came and went without the arrival of the much-needed supplies. The ongoing delays prompted Newman to contact Lennox and Burgess a week later, saying "a large number of men engaged at Cape Hatteras . . . will soon have nothing to do but eat the rations furnished by the Government."

Finally, in December, Lennox and Burgess secured three schooners for the project. Two of the boats were loaded with the long-overdue supplies, and by the end of the month they were on their way to Cape Hatteras.

With the much-needed supplies on hand at last, work progressed rapidly at the site. At a point six hundred feet northeast of the 1803 tower, Stetson had his men excavate a wide hole six feet deep. Although his original instruction called for pilings to be driven into the floor of the pit, Stetson found the compact sand so hard that he could only drive a metal test rod a little more than six feet down. Feeling the ground would be sturdy enough to support the weight of the massive tower, Stetson requested and received permission to do away with the pilings. Instead, he drew upon the inherent nature of the Outer Banks to implement a decidedly different approach to the foundation.

Barrier islands such as Hatteras contain a shallow freshwater aquifer not far below the surface of the ground. Realizing the bottom of his foundation hole was underneath the surface of the freshwater lens and that wood completely submerged in freshwater is resistant to decay, Stetson decided to exploit the island's geology.

He placed a wooden cofferdam around the excavated work site and employed "powerful steam pumps" to remove the water inside. Next he had three courses of four-by-six-inch yellow pine placed crosswise on top of one another. In the center of the hole, where the pine courses intersected, he then placed granite rubble and other stone scraps to begin the stone footers for the tower. Once the stone foundation had been carried up above the level of the freshwater water table, Stetson removed the walls of the cofferdam, submerging the pine planks, and later back-filled around

the foundation walls. The planks, submerged in an underwater anaerobic environment, were buried under tons of sand.

Ironically, the construction site had never been officially approved by the Light-House Board. A change in district engineers had resulted in the oversight, which was not realized until the following spring. Newman, the former engineer, had left his position before the project had cleared official channels, and his replacement, a man named Simpson, assumed that everything had been arranged when he took over the assignment.

Although Simpson agreed with Newman's selection of the site, the Light-House Board nonetheless assigned a committee to visit Hatteras Island in May 1869 and review the situation. Luckily, the group agreed with Newman and Simpson's conclusions and approved the placement of Stetson's tower, which was by then well underway and clearly visible to all.

Meanwhile, six feet below the surface, Stetson began the massive octagonal foundation that would be the base of the tower. Closer to the surface, plinth courses of cut granite were placed, and above them brick panels and cut granite quoins gave the bottom of the Cape Hatteras Lighthouse its classic design. Construction of the base was completed by the end of 1869.

Simpson had hoped that the work would be further along, but delays caused by continuing problems with Lennox and Burgess and the time-consuming nature of the transportation of materials made it impossible for Stetson's crew to stay on schedule. In addition, another familiar problem—sickness—again affected the workmen at the Hatteras site.

A number of Stetson's men became ill with complaints similar to those that had struck Dearborn's men. Five workers were sent

Although originally designed for one of the assistant keepers, lighthouse officials decided to assign the new quarters to the principal keeper instead. U.S. Lighthouse Service photographer H. Bamber captured this image in 1893 while documenting light stations in the South. Bamber always included the keepers and their families in his photographs. At one time the National Park Service used the structure for VIP quarters, and in the 1950s it was used as a retreat for government officials. During an era when a distinction was made between buildings used for official business and those for other purposes, the quarters were painted pink. Locals still refer to the house, long since repainted, as the Pink House.

Bamber also photographed the double keepers quarters in 1893. Common to several Outer Banks lighthouses is the white fence surrounding the living quarters to keep out free-range livestock. It was called "double" because it housed as many as three assistant keepers and their families. From 1856 until 1906 the third keeper tended the Hatteras beacon on the cape, which was a mile south of the lighthouse.

home from the site in August 1869 to recuperate, all bearing many of the classic symptoms of malaria. Stetson and others at the site suspected a rancid pond under the keepers quarters might be responsible. Stetson asked for permission to drain the pond and fill the area with sand, but the Light-House Board rejected his request. Instead he was told to fill only the area under the keepers quarters with sand and do no more. Stetson complied. In reality, it is unlikely that, considering the countless places on Hatteras Island in which mosquitoes could breed, filling a single water source would have had much effect on the mosquito problem.

Although work on the pond was not approved, unplanned renovation work on the keepers quarters was. The inspection team that visited the site two months earlier had found the dwelling to be in "wretched condition" and authorized an allocation of $1,000 to make the necessary repairs.

Work on the tower progressed rapidly in 1870, due in part to the large pool of Hatteras Island day laborers from which Stetson was able to draw. As many as a hundred local workers jumped at the opportunity to make as much as $1.50 per day, a princely sum for the islanders at the time.

There were plenty of bricks to haul as the masons slowly built their way into the air. They laid a pair of circular brick walls, one inside the other with a hollow space in between. At intervals they joined the walls with radial brick masonry. As the tower took shape, nine landings, placed on either side of the tower, began to fill the interior. Each landing also had a window, providing natural illumination and a peek at the receding ground.

The tower went up at an impressive rate. By the end of January, it was 50 feet above the first floor. At the end of March it was nearly 100 feet off the ground; by the middle of June, it was 153½ feet above the ground—as tall as its predecessor 600 feet away—and still climbing.

Stetson then stopped work on the tower and sent most of his crew home while he waited for job-specific alterations to be made by the iron manufacturer. He kept a skeleton crew of six men to serve as watchmen for the site. The alterations were completed by

---

While the planners of Stetson's tower may have prepared against the battering weather brought by the hurricanes and nor'easters that frequent the Outer Banks, they could not have foreseen some of the other natural phenomena that have affected the Cape Hatteras Lighthouse.

On April 17, 1879, a severe storm rolled over Hatteras Island, bringing fierce lightning and drenching rains. The tower received a direct hit from the lightning, which inspectors later attributed to poor grounding on the part of the original work crew. They remedied the problem by burying an iron disk at the base of the tower and connecting it to the ironwork in the tower with a metal rod. While this might have protected the lighthouse from additional strikes, the damage had already been done. Within two months the keeper noticed several long thin cracks on the interior brick wall of the lighthouse tower. Those cracks, although mended by masons, are still visible along portions of the tower's interior walls.

The second natural event to impact the lighthouse occurred on August 31, 1886, when an earthquake centered near Charleston, South Carolina, rocked the Outer Banks and gave the Hatteras light a good shaking.

According to the official report of the incident, the trembler was nothing to scoff at, especially for the keepers who found themselves nearly two hundred feet above the ground when it arrived. The following account of the incident was taken from Light-House Board reports for 1886:

The keeper reports that he felt an earthquake shock on Aug. 31, at 9.50 p.m. local time. The shock lasted from ten to fifteen seconds. It was accompanied by a rumbling noise. There were four shocks. They were severe enough to slightly crack the storm panes in the lantern tower. The second shock occurred at 10 o'clock, lasted about 6 seconds, and was very light. The third shock occurred at 10.07, lasted about ten seconds, and was moderate. The fourth shock occurred at 10.29 and lasted about six seconds, and was very light. Its force was sufficient to set suspended objects swinging and to overthrow light objects. He further states that it sounded like a rumbling noise coming up the tower.

Then the tower would tremble and sway backward and forward like a tree shaken by the wind. The shock was so strong that we could not keep our backs against the parapet wall. It would throw us right from it. The swinging was from northeast to southwest.

On September 3 another slight shock was felt at 11.05 p.m., which lasted about three seconds.

Cracks in the interior wall were the only evidence of damage from these incidents. Stetson's tower proved steady as a rock, which may be more than could be said for the keepers' nerves as they clung to the swaying tower that shaky night in August 1886.

This turn-of-the-century photograph of the Cape Hatteras Light Station, probably taken by Lighthouse Service photographer H. Bamber, provides a classic image of the days when keepers tended the station. These men and their families were part of the dedicated group of approximately five thousand keepers and their families who manned more than one thousand light stations along America's coasts and the Great Lakes.

The base of the 1803 tower, on the horizon to the right, is partially hidden by the double keepers quarters. The pond in the foreground appears to be at flood stage due to natural overwash.

mid-September, and Simpson dispatched a working party to the site to begin the final installation work. Iron parts for the lantern work continued to arrive throughout the month of October, and by the end of November the lantern was complete and ready for the lens.

On November 19, Simpson ordered district lampist George Crosman Jr. to Hatteras to remove the old lens and install the new one. Crosman set up the lens, fine-tuned the revolving machinery, performed a test run to make sure everything was operational, and removed the old lens for shipment to the Staten Island lighthouse depot. Sometime in December 1870, the tallest beacon in the country began to blink its brilliant warning across Diamond Shoals.

Workmen completed the project by whitewashing the interior of the tower and painting the exterior to serve as a day marker. The Light-House Board wanted to maintain the same red-over-white color pattern the first tower had displayed since 1854. Day-mark changes were significant, and each change was accompanied by official, well-circulated notices from officials of the board. Altering the markings might create dangerous confusion for mariners who had not been informed of a new color scheme.

Accordingly, the board directed that the tower should be painted in a brick-colored wash and that the granite base should be left its natural gray color, to again form a lighter column against the green vegetative background. While there is still some debate about the exact nature of the colorings of the exterior for the first two years after its completion, one thing is agreed: For a brief period the Cape Hatteras Lighthouse stood just as it does now, but without its famous black-and-white pattern. That was not to come for another three years.

With the tower nearly complete, some of the workmen erected an iron fence on a granite base around its perimeter to keep the free-range cows and pigs from entering the lighthouse, and others began construction of another single keepers house at the light station. In November 1870 Stetson requested permission to use some of the leftover materials from the lighthouse to construct a dwelling, saying the double keepers quarters was too small to house the three families that were living there. Board officials approved the request and sent Stetson a set of plans.

By the middle of March, work on the new quarters had been completed. Simpson directed Stetson to again select a skeleton guard crew and send the remaining workers home. Although Stetson and the work crew were scheduled to move north to Bodie Island to begin construction on the new lighthouse there, the project was delayed by a property transfer.

Finally, in June, Simpson directed that workmen move their quarters, mess room, the tram railroad, the other structures on the site, and the scows north to the new work site. Aside from the addition of a small oil house near the base of the light, the Cape Hatteras Light Station was complete.

The new light performed marvelously. A clocklike mechanism, wound from the top, allowed iron weights to descend slowly through the center of the lighthouse. The moving mechanism in turn rotated the wonderfully intricate first-order Fresnel lens, which projected a flash visible twenty miles out to sea.

Although the lighthouse performed well at night, the Light-House Board began to feel the brick-colored wash was not an effective day mark. In March 1873 the board approved a plan giving the Hatteras light its distinctive stripes. It also ordered that Cape Lookout be painted in a checkered design and Bodie Island in stripes. By the end of the summer, all three were displaying the distinctive markings that have endured to the present.

5

THE
UNKNOWN BUILDER

AN ENIGMATIC CARPENTER AND HOUSEWRIGHT

WHEN THE NEW LIGHTHOUSE stood finished, Dexter Stetson moved on to the other construction sites at Bodie Island and Currituck Beach and then disappeared into relative obscurity, at least from the perspective of the island inhabitants. Like most artists, he attempted to leave his name on his work by installing a small plaque. The plaque, however, was removed in 1874. As a result, little was known about the man who was behind three of the seven most well-known lighthouses in North Carolina.

Over time, as the lighthouse came to be treasured by a wider audience than the seamen who navigated by its light, people have wondered about the man who facilitated the construction. Many presumed that, like the workers who laid the brick and wielded the paintbrushes, he was from the area, maybe not an islander but surely a southerner. They were surprised to learn that he was a carpenter from New England.

The mists of time, like the fog that regularly lifts over Diamond Shoals, have only recently parted to reveal something of Stetson. Cape Hatteras National Seashore historian F. Ross Holland Jr. first wrote of Stetson in 1968 when he compiled a history of the light station. What little he related about the man behind the lighthouse was drawn from the files of the Lighthouse Board Fifth District Engineer Letter Press, part of Record Group 26 of the U.S. Lighthouse Service.

"Much of the correspondence was lost," Holland said recently. "A fire in the Department of Commerce in 1920 destroyed much of the old Lighthouse Service records." Indeed many details of what went on during the building of the Cape Hatteras Lighthouse were noted only in indexed letters to and from Stetson, as foreman of construction, and his superior, J. H. Simpson, engineer of the Fifth District. The extant letters barely survived the fire and are charred around the edges.

In 1980 David Stick, the renowned historian of the Outer Banks, also wrote about Stetson and described him as "a man ingenious enough to figure new ways of getting things done and capable of doing them." In Stick's book, *North Carolina Lighthouses,* he emphasized Stetson's resourcefulness in solving the dilemma surrounding the design of the foundation without using pilings and his ability to work around the late arrivals of building materials.

In recent years, as interest in the Cape Hatteras Lighthouse swelled with news of the plans to move it to a new site, filmmaker Kevin Duffus's researches while gathering material for a documentary on the lighthouse led him to Lynn, Massachusetts, where he found Stetson's grave. Sandy Clunies, a certified genealogist researching Record Group 26 at the National Archives, discovered letters and other documents that helped fill in most of the picture of the man behind the Cape Hatteras Lighthouse.

STETSON WAS BORN NOVEMBER 8, 1815, in Durham, Maine, to Charles Stetson of Scituate, Massachusetts, and his wife, Abigail, of Freeport, Maine. One source claims that Dexter was born in Freeport, which bordered on Durham at the time. Charles and Abigail had seven children: two daughters—Asenath and Almira—and five sons—Charles C., Washington, Albert, Dexter, and Solomon.

As a youth Dexter was known for his love of nature and a penchant for roaming, traits he was said to have inherited from his father. "He lived in Durham, just one town in from the water," Margaret Wentworth of the Durham Historical Society pointed out in the strong accent of the region. "He lived in a small town adjacent to Brunswick and Freeport, only a short distance from the Portland Head and Hendricks Head lights. Dexter was surrounded by shipbuilding. In fact, an ancient road, called the

Shortly after marrying, Dexter Stetson and his wife ran a boardinghouse in Nahant, Massachusetts. The home was one of many owned by his wife's family and was known as the Abner Hood Jr. house.

'Mast Road,' went right through Durham. There are still traces of it today after winter leaves. Back then logs were carried from inland—and Durham has always been heavily wooded, it's part of the great Northeastern Woods. They made up the masts of the magnificent sailing vessels, but they had to pass down this road. Dexter would have seen this every day he lived here."

Stetson's family members worked with their hands, and he likewise earned the documented title "housewright." He might have acquired a love for shaping wood while watching the deft shipbuilders coax straight pieces of raw wood into the sleek curves of a ship's bow and stern. At the same time, people all around him were making their living from the sea.

He hauled logs in 1840 and erected a fashionable log cabin in Nahant for a friend during the presidential election when cabins and hard cider were symbolic of the supporters of John Tyler's bid for the White House. It is likely that memories of a grandfather's log cabin influenced his building, but Stetson demonstrated an artistic touch when he installed diamond-paned windows.

In the 1840s Stetson moved to Lynn, Massachusetts, northeast of Boston. The town had a population of several thousand, and its primary industry was shoe manufacturing. In such a setting, a carpenter stood out from the masses.

On July 6, 1846, he married Ann Maria Hood of Nahant—a peninsula off of Lynn—whose family was influential in the area

At the age of twenty-six, Stetson built this fashionable log cottage for a friend in 1840, a time when cabins and cottages were symbolic of those who supported the candidacy of John Tyler for president. Some have speculated that Stetson based the building on memories of a similar cottage in which his grandfather lived. Stetson demonstrated his own artistic touch by installing diamond-paned windows, which can be seen along the right side of the cottage in this image. Aside from his construction skills, the political aspect of this home should not be overlooked. Stetson was enmeshed in local politics and no doubt capitalized on political ties in gaining appointment as a building contractor for the government.

and had significant real estate holdings. The new couple operated a boardinghouse on some property Stetson purchased from his in-laws. Their only child was born on April 4, 1847, in Nahant, and her name was Helen Louise.

After Stetson settled in Nahant, he joined John Hammond, an old friend from Maine, in forming a construction business. They were credited with building the "finest summer cottages Nahant proudly claimed," according to Stanley C. Paterson and Carl Seaburg in a 1991 article written for the Nahant Historical Society.

Stetson's reputation may have been made in 1851 in Nahant when he was credited with building the original village church on the Nahant road in Lynn. It was a nondenominational meetinghouse, and the task carried a heavy responsibility in the community. The construction job was a prestigious project, and its completion won Stetson the community's respect.

"It was built so well for $2,258 that part of a Sunday sermon included praise for Stetson on his handiwork," observed Calantha Sears of the Nahant Historical Society. The village church still stands today, minus its tower and clock, as a private residence.

Shortly after constructing the church, Stetson was elected a selectman for Nahant, a position roughly comparable to that of commissioner. At the time the political situation in Lynn was emotionally charged with talk that the Nahant area wanted to separate from Lynn and organize as a separate town. The town was established in 1853, and Stetson and Hammond played roles as two of Nahant's twenty-eight founding fathers. Stetson's high profile also won him some influential contacts in both the state and federal governments.

Within sight of Stetson's boardinghouse, a lighthouse was being built in 1855 at Egg Rock in Nahant. Stetson came to know the foreman of the construction and even labored at the site himself.

In the late 1850s Stetson began to bid on federal construction projects and won a contract for work on some storehouses and wharves in New Orleans. He was there in 1861 when war broke out between the states. Stetson made his way back to the Northeast with a valise of Federal gold that he had to return to the government.

After the war Stetson's New England roots worked to his advantage in securing government contracts for construction work in the South. Most southerner builders at the time were not allowed to bid on government projects due to a whiplash effect of their service to the South during the war. Lighthouse construction in the South kept Stetson busy for several years.

When W. J. Newman chose Stetson to be the construction foreman at Cape Hatteras, he knew that he was entrusting the task to a man known for high standards of workmanship who had the skills of a carpenter and a housewright and who also possessed an intimate knowledge of lighthouse construction. As soon as the appropriation was made for the new tower at Cape Hatteras, Stetson sailed for North Carolina and set up shop in Buxton.

Stetson played many roles during the work on the island, from troubleshooter to construction boss. One load of granite boulders was lost in the Pamlico Sound, and Stetson wrote Washington requesting a replacement shipment. None was sent. "Go get it," was the official response. Until recently it has been supposed that Stetson did just that; however, excavation around the lighthouse during the relocation work revealed that he likely "filled in" with

In 1878 Stetson remodeled a former steamship terminal into his own home. He retrieved the diamond-paned windows from the cottage he had built in 1840 and installed them in the new home, calling it Black Rock Cottage. Stetson is the gentleman on the porch. The woman in the carriage is probably his daughter, Helen Louise, and the three women on the porch likely include his two sisters-in-law, Amelia and Julia Hood.

other types of rocks obtained locally. Islanders have claimed that the original load of granite remained at the bottom of Pamlico Sound, and its whereabouts have been passed down from generation to generation.

After the work was finished at Hatteras, Stetson was ordered in 1870 to break down his workers barracks, mess room, blacksmith shop, and the other outbuildings and reassemble them forty miles to the north and begin work on the next coastal light at Bodie Island. The result there, like that he left behind at Cape Hatteras, was one of America's classic light stations.

After completing the work at Bodie Island, he supervised the work at Currituck Beach, which was based on plans identical to the Bodie Island tower. Some have speculated that he returned to Nahant in 1873 to care for his ailing wife, Ann Maria. She died on August 4, 1874. His thirty-year career as a foreman of federal construction projects seems to have ended in 1876. His lighthouse work possibly continued into the next decade. An 1880 census listed him as a lighthouse superintendent.

STETSON'S LEGACY STANDS ON the shore of Cape Hatteras in the form of a lighthouse taller than any before it. Joe Jakubik of International Chimney Corporation, Inc., supervised the March 1992 restoration of the Hatteras lighthouse. "He knew his stuff," Jakubik observed. "For instance, in those days, cast iron could only be made to within one-sixteenth of an inch per foot tolerance. With more than 265 steps to install, Stetson could have been off by 16¾ inches by the time he reached the top. Instead, each piece was filed perfectly so that the stairway neatly reached every landing, and the total height was correct.

"The brick column, including all windows and doors, were probably constructed prior to the stairway," Jakubik noted. "Near the top, between the service room and the gallery level the staircase almost interfered with one of the three service room windows. Because the window's location was dictated by the orientation of the gallery brackets, Stetson solved the potential fit-up problem by cropping out part of the vent above the affected window so as to be almost unnoticeable.

"And consider," Jakubik continued, "they laid radial brick then to form a conical-shaped building." This posed an interesting challenge for the men constructing the double walls, which had radiating spokes of bricks between them for strength. "They were laying brick in a circle and tapering in," Jakubik added. "They had to maintain a circle, but no matter

The only plaque at the Hatteras lighthouse gives the barest information about the building of the structure. Stetson placed a plaque bearing his name on the tower, but it was removed when it was deemed inappropriate.

how carefully they laid the brick toward the upper part of the tower, without highly accurate measuring instruments, the brick laid at the gallery deck area turned out slightly oval."

While analyzing the brickwork of the tower, Jakubik imagined how Stetson might have organized his bricklaying crew. Comparing the laying of brick in a circle to cutting an orange, he noted that while slicing in one direction the hope is that the cut meets at the same place when the circle is finished. Likely Stetson had at least six right-handed bricklayers and at least one left-handed bricklayer so that the row was level when it was completed.

"But what do you do with the extra mortar on the trowel after scraping off the excess after each brick was placed? Throw it to the ground?" Jakubik asked. "And what if you're a hundred or more feet above ground? Stetson was the type of boss who wouldn't let his men just sling the extra mortar on the ground," he pointed out. "So how did they get rid of it? Between the double walls. When we dropped a line we discovered extra material between the walls that was about three feet tall."

When planning the restoration of the lighthouse, Jakubik ordered a full-sized template of the newly cast gallery iron deck plates. After he had placed the template on the existing deck, he said, "I lined them up and had to get a center point on the brackets and nothing fit! Each of the new ones would have to be cast individually using varying dimensions. In 1870 the blacksmith's shop would have had to preassemble the original plates to fit a circular shape, and Stetson would have had to make them fit on the oval brick column by grinding. He also made them fit by filling with material in between the splices on the deck plates. I've never seen this material."

Another discovery was made about the iron decking during the restoration work. Jakubik observed, "Each plate was identified with Roman numerals, and according to how the plates were placed, we found that the numerals were backward; that is, I, II, III, VI, V, IV, IIV, IIIV, etc." Nevertheless, the pieces fit precisely and have withstood the punishment of time and the harsh nature of the storms of the Outer Banks. Considering the workmanship noted during the restoration work, Jakubik estimated, "The production of the deck plates alone would be worth $100,000 today."

Dexter Stetson, foreman of the construction of the 1870 Cape Hatteras Lighthouse, overcame numerous engineering problems in completing his task. The result is one of the most recognized lighthouses in America, now designated a National Historic Landmark. Stetson went on to oversee the construction of the Bodie Island and the Currituck Beach Lighthouses.

For years no one knew what Stetson looked like, but recently this engraving was discovered in Auburn, Maine. This is the first time it has been published in this century.

STETSON LIVED THE REST of his life in Nahant. In 1878 he moved a former steamship terminal to a site across from the Black Rock Wharf. He remodeled it into the house in which he lived until his death. Revisiting part of his past, Stetson retrieved the diamond-paned windows from the cabin he had built for his friend in 1840 and installed them in his new home. He named it Black Rock Cottage, and it overlooked the harbor at Lynn.

In 1895 Stetson suffered a "paralytic shock that left him incapacitated and an invalid," according to a newspaper in Lynn. His daughter, Helen Louise, and two sisters-in-law, Julia and Amelia Hood, cared for him during the final four years of his life. Some said that his "death came as a blessing on December 1, 1899." As for his living far beyond the expected lifespan for a man born in the early 1800s and reaching the age of eighty-four, Margaret Wentworth of the Durham Historical Society said, "If a person survived childhood and the [Civil] War, s/he had a good chance at longevity." Stetson's grandfather, Elijah, lived to be ninety-nine years old, for instance. Wentworth added, "New Englanders were all farmers and fishermen and lumbermen, and that is good healthy work."

As a testimony to Stetson's building acumen, Black Rock Cottage still stands today. The resourceful carpenter himself rests in the Pine Grove Cemetery on Larch Avenue in Lynn, alongside his wife and their only daughter. In recent years the grave of the once obscure lighthouse builder has had more visitors than usual as part of tours sponsored by the Nahant Historical Society.

6

OTHER LIGHTS AT CAPE HATTERAS

FLOATING LIGHTHOUSES AND DEEP-WATER RIGS

THE DEGREE OF SUCCESS enjoyed by the 1870 Cape Hatteras Lighthouse far outshone the failure of its predecessor. Yet even with a taller tower and the incomparable Fresnel lens transmitting the beacon farther out to sea than any that had illuminated these waters before, the dangers were not completely removed from the shipping lanes near Hatteras Island. Lurking beneath the surface of these waters was the shallow stretch of sea known as Diamond Shoals.

Mariners referred to Diamond Shoals with awe and keen awareness of the expert seamanship—and to some extent good fortune—needed to avoid wrecking on these undulating underwater sand traps. Three distinct ridges of shifting sand lie in wait for any vessel that ventures too close to the Cape Hatteras shoreline.

The area surrounding Cape Hatteras is a kind of intersection of two water highways passing through the area. The colder, faster current is a remnant of an arctic flow from the northeast that hugs the shoreline and flows in a southerly direction. Ships trying to take advantage of this fast lane have to stay close in toward shore. Such navigation is a game for only the hearty, though, because

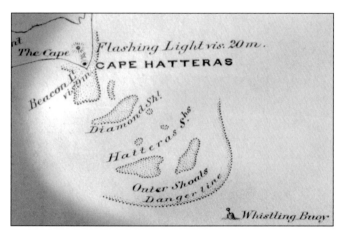

An 1880s map published by the U.S. Lifesaving Service shows the Cape Hatteras Lighthouse marking the notorious Diamond Shoals for large vessels. The Hatteras Beacon's position is also noted for ships navigating the sloughs between the shoals in front of the cape and for local coasting vessels slipping into Pamlico Sound via an inner channel. At the time of this map, only a "whistling buoy" marked the outer limits of the shoals.

many who attempted it ended up in dire straits before finishing the journey past Cape Hatteras.

To the west is the Gulf Stream, which creates a warm path in its northerly flow. If each current remained parallel to the other, weather conditions would remain calmer with smoother transitions between the seasons. But this is not the case. The cold water from the north and the warm gulf water battle constantly as their courses wander into one another at Cape Hatteras. Fog and sudden storms form with robust winds and mountainous waves. The warm waters of the gulf feed the fury of hurricanes howling off the west coast of Africa or Caribbean coasts, driving the engines of these dangerous and unpredictable storms.

The 1803 Cape Hatteras Lighthouse was not of much assistance to mariners navigating these shoals, because the light from the tower was not always visible to them. By 1806 Congress ordered a feasibility study of building a light "on the tip of Hatteras Shoals, which have been long a terror to navigators." The survey team found that it was not advisable to build a lighthouse on Diamond Shoals because the ocean bottom was made of loose and shifting sand. The survey also reported that the prevailing winds, waves, and tidal currents created an environment too harsh to maintain a lighthouse.

To extend the light of the Cape Hatteras Lighthouse, the original tower was extended to 150 feet in 1854 and then replaced by a 198-foot tower in 1870. Even so, at its best the beam from the light station could be seen nineteen miles from shore, and that was usually too close to Diamond Shoals. After all, the mariners did not want to see the Cape Hatteras Lighthouse; they wanted to see it on the horizon so they knew they were a safe distance from Outer Diamond Shoals.

Since the shoals reach so far out into the Atlantic, seamen had a great deal of difficulty judging what was a safe distance from shore by using only the Cape Hatteras Lighthouse as a point of reference. In the early nineteenth century the U.S. lighthouse service experimented with a variety of devices to "bell the cat." In 1822 buoys were moored to strategic points along the shoals, but many of these drifted from their moorings and misled the mariners. Some of the wayward buoys drifted into the Gulf of Mexico, and others traveled as far east as Europe.

LIGHTSHIPS

In 1824 a lightship was stationed on Diamond Shoals. Moored to the sandy bottom at the edge of the inner shoals, the Cape Hatteras lightship stood its vigil and beamed a warning to passing ships until June 1827 when a storm tore the 320-ton vessel from its mooring and pushed it toward shore.

Over the next seventy years lighthouse officials attempted to moor other lightships on the shoals, but one by one those vessels became stranded on the beaches of Cape Hatteras. George Putnam, commissioner of lighthouses from 1912 to 1934, again referred to Diamond Shoals as the Graveyard of the Atlantic.

In the late 1880s merchants and mariners pressed Congress for appropriate funds for a lighthouse to be built on the shoals. In his book *Ancient and Modern Light-Houses* (1888), Maj. D. P. Heap of the Army Corps of Engineers detailed a plan for building a lighthouse on Diamond Shoals. Heap's plan advised anchoring the offshore tower with a steel or cast-iron caisson that was forty-five feet in diameter. The caisson would be sunk into the sandy ocean floor, and then a double-walled tower would be built atop this sturdy foundation. Riprap placed around the base would provide additional protection from storm surges.

Heap's plans included an ominous and somewhat prophetic warning: "Should a storm overtake the cylinder while being towed to the site, it would, in all probability, be lost, and the same catastrophe might occur if there were a heavy blow during the first part of the sinking of the cylinder." He also predicted the price of the

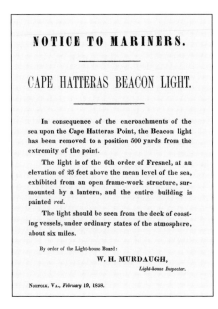

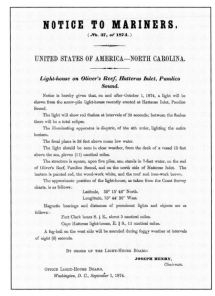

Changing the location of navigational aids or the addition or removal of a lighted marker was a serious matter for seamen. Formal notices were prepared and well circulated in advance of any such changes. In 1858 the Light-House Board published an announcement on the moving of the beacon at Hatteras (far left). In 1874 a small screw-pile lighthouse was erected at the south end of Hatteras Island to mark the inlet to Pamlico Sound.

proposed lighthouse: "Barring accidents, the cost should not exceed $300,000 for the foundation, but I would not be safe to commence work without having at least $500,000 available."

Although engineers had successfully built lighthouses in the Atlantic at Minots Ledge off the coast of Massachusetts and at Eddystone off the coast of England, the soft sands of Diamond Shoals presented a unique problem. The clash of cold and warm currents transformed the sand into a "fluid," and it flowed in the direction of the constantly changing winds and waves. So there was no stable ocean floor to hold the anchoring caisson in the shoals.

Despite these seemingly insurmountable obstacles, the U.S. Light-House Board decided to proceed with the Diamond Shoals lighthouse project. Congress authorized a tempting $500,000 appropriation, and officials opened bids on July 1, 1890. Three contractors—Anderson and Barr, Theodore Cooper and Company, and William Sooy Smith—submitted plans for building a cast-iron tower lined with brick, a lighthouse that closely resembled the one Heap had described in his 1888 book. All three bids came within the cost estimated by Heap and appropriated by Congress.

The Light-House Board chose one of the three contractors (unfortunately the name was not included in existing records) and authorized $200,000 to start the project. The contractor had a fifty-four-foot-wide, forty-five-foot-tall caisson constructed in Norfolk, Virginia, and transported to Diamond Shoals in 1891.

Three plans were submitted to the Light-House Board in 1890 for a navigational guide to be built on Diamond Shoals. From left to right, these are the plans proposed by William Sooy Smith (at a cost of $488,325), Theodore Cooper and Company ($474,000), and Anderson and Barr ($485,000). Construction was begun on the project, but ocean currents and a storm destroyed the first effort to establish a foundation for the lighthouse and the plans were scrapped.

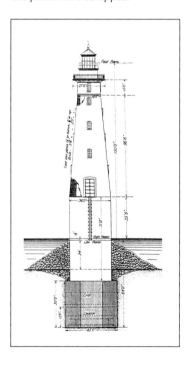
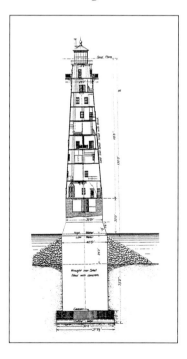
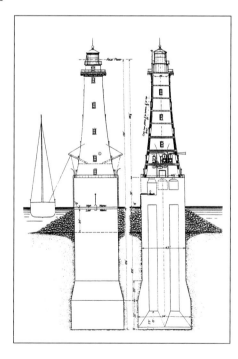

Capt. Albert F. Eells of Boston came up with the last proposal for building a lighthouse on Diamond Shoals. His plan was presented in the June 11, 1904, issue of the *Scientific American,* which included this illustration. Eells had enough political clout to get a bill passed in Congress in support of his plan. According to the agreement, Eells would have been handsomely rewarded had he followed through with the building of this tower, planned to reach an impressive two hundred feet above the sea. The contract, however, required Eells to make the initial investment himself, which may have rendered the project too risky in Eells's opinion and it was never attempted.

After the water-filled caisson was lowered into place, about twenty-five feet below the surface of the Atlantic, pumps emptied it so workers could begin building the foundation for a tower that would rise 150 feet above sea level and hold a first-order Fresnel lens.

Within a week, however, ocean currents had undermined the caisson's foothold in the sand, and a storm washed away the remnants of the first attempt to claim "permanent" anchorage on Diamond Shoals. The plan was scrapped, and lighthouse officials used the remaining appropriation to cover part of the cost of building Light Vessel (LV) 69, which was to be stationed on the shoals.

In 1894 the Light-House Board approved a second ambitious endeavor to build a lighthouse on Diamond Shoals. This time the plan called for a skeletal iron tower on iron pilings, reminiscent of the Florida reef lighthouses designed by Gen. George Gordon Meade. This plan was abandoned only a short time later and never attempted.

In 1904 one last attempt was made to erect an offshore lighthouse at Cape Hatteras. Capt. Albert F. Eells of Boston had studied the first two attempts and proposed another solution to anchoring a tower on the shifting sands of Diamond Shoals. The captain evidently had enough political clout to get H.R. Bill No.

7:264 passed, which gave him "an opportunity to build a lighthouse at his own expense. . . . Under the terms of the bill he is authorized to construct a substantial, sufficient lighthouse and fog signal of the most improved construction, together with auxiliary works of the most modern character and such as will be necessary to maintain the same permanently at the outer side of the outer Diamond shoal [*sic*] on the coast of North Carolina, at Cape Hatteras."

Eells's plan called for a lighthouse that rose a lofty two hundred feet from a foundation that reached sixty feet below the high-water level. A seventy-five-foot-wide foundation had "whale fins" to give it extra footing in the sandy ocean floor.

After the lighthouse was built, Eells was to be paid $590,000, a handsome reward, but with some strings attached. "When the structure is completed Capt. Eells is required to maintain it and the light for one year at his own expense. The Lighthouse Board then operates it for four years at the government's expense. If the lighthouse is then approved and accepted by the Secretary of Commerce and Labor, the United States is authorized to pay Capt. Eells the sum of $590,000."

Eells did not build his lighthouse or receive his promised fortune despite the fact that Congress increased the appropriation to a tantalizing sum of $750,000. Waiting for five years to collect his reward with the initial costs all coming from his personal funds discouraged Eells from undertaking the risky project.

A series of lightships were stationed at Diamond Shoals. All were emblazoned with the same name along the hull. In 1899 this Diamond Shoals lightship washed ashore near Hatteras after a hurricane severed its mooring chain and blew the vessel toward shore. LV 69 was repaired and refloated and returned to its station.

In September 1897 Light Vessel 69, appropriately named *Diamond Shoals*, assumed its watery post about 8 miles and 128 degrees from Cape Hatteras Lighthouse. This feisty lightship successfully stuck to its moorings and proved tough enough to withstand the wind and waves. In his 1913 book *Lightships and Lighthouses*, Frederick A. Talbot described what the crew aboard the *Diamond Shoals* faced on a daily basis.

> The light-vessel controlled by the United States which occupies the most responsible and perilous post is the Diamond Shoal, off Cape Hatteras. It throws its warning rays from a spot about four and five-eighths miles beyond the most seaward point of this terrible ocean graveyard, and is thirteen and five-eighth miles distant from Cape Hatteras light on the mainland. A long way from the actual danger spot, you say, but the little squad of men who have to maintain the light through storm and calm will tell you that . . . in 180 feet of water . . . there is the ever-present danger of anchors being dragged, or of the craft breaking adrift under the force of the cyclonic disturbances which ravage this sinister coast. . . . Probably this is the most dangerous station on the whole seaboard and if any heavy trouble is caused by the tempest, the Diamond Shoal inevitably bears grim evidence of the conflict. The skill of the [lightship] engineers is taxed sorely to devise ways and means of keeping the vessel in the position she is designed to occupy, but moorings and anchors must be of great weight and strength to stand up against a wind blowing eighty miles an hour, with the

This Diamond Shoals lightship (LV 71) was sunk by a German U-boat during World War I after the vessel's crew radioed a warning of the submarine's presence along the Outer Banks.

waves running "mountains high" and repeatedly sweeping the vessel from stem to stern.

Lightship crews often described their tour of duty as "imprisonment," with only seasickness to break the tedium. They usually served four months on and four months off, and the turnover was high. The hardy men who manned the first *Diamond Shoals*—and the other Diamond Shoals lightships that followed it—performed an invaluable service by saving countless lives and cargoes from the Graveyard of the Atlantic. U.S. Lighthouse Service logs show that in 1899 alone 5,146 vessels successfully navigated the shoals with the aid of the lightship.

While lightships served on Diamond Shoals, twenty-two storms hit and dragged the vessels off station or blew them adrift. For two years the first *Diamond Shoals* held its ground, alternating with Light Vessel 71 when it needed repairs. Then the inevitable happened.

In 1899 a monstrous hurricane hit. After the storm subsided, lookout F. J. Rollinson of the Creeds Hill Lifesaving Station spotted a ship beached about a mile to the southwest, roughly three and a half miles south of the Cape Hatteras Lighthouse. When the surfmen reached the stranded vessel they saw *Diamond Shoals* emblazoned on its side. The hurricane winds had dragged it to shore from its mooring, but all nine crewmen had survived and were rescued by breeches buoy. The surfmen had to rescue the lightship's crew several more times during the salvage operations, but the crew was undaunted in their efforts to float the lightship back to its station on Outer Diamond Shoals.

The first *Diamond Shoals* faithfully continued its lonely vigil until 1901. Light Vessels 71 and 72 replaced it and stood watch on Outer Diamond Shoals from 1901 until 1918.

A lightship is simply a floating lighthouse, but as was proved when a lightship was rammed by the *John Bossert*, lightships can also be targets. Passing ships were often reprimanded for passing too close to a lightship, causing not only a great deal of anxiety but also fatalities. The *Diamond Shoals* light vessel was especially vulnerable because it marked the channel between Outer Diamond Shoals and the Gulf Stream, a fast lane for northbound ships. Lightship duty was full of risks and sacrifice, and LV 71 made the ultimate sacrifice to earn a special place in seafaring history.

On the afternoon of August 8, 1918, first mate Walter Barnett made one of the most difficult decisions of his life. His captain was on shore leave, and Barnett, who had recently transferred to LV 71, was in charge when a German submarine began firing on a

The last Diamond Shoals lightship was launched in Bay City, Michigan, on October 15, 1946. Built to be tough, this lightship had thick sides and hulls to withstand the punishment of mountainous waves or the possibility of collision with passing ships. Ship captains were frequently reprimanded for failure to steer clear of lightships. As an additional step in making these vessels more visible at sea, lightships were traditionally painted red.

merchant ship about a mile and a half away. The Germans reportedly warned the crew of LV 71 that if they broadcast the submarine's position, LV 71 would be sunk. To emphasize their warning, the Germans reportedly fired six shots at the lightship.

News reporter Aycock Brown wrote that as the U-boat turned away to pursue the merchant ship, Barnett broadcast the submarine's position. Some accounts estimated that a convoy of thirty-five ships picked up Barnett's broadcast and took refuge in the harbor at Beaufort, North Carolina. The submarine returned to Diamond Shoals and sank LV 71 with gunfire. The lightship crew escaped in boats, and after watching their doomed vessel go to the bottom, the men floated safely to shore.

Although lightship duty during stormy weather on Diamond Shoals was less dangerous than during wartime, it still demanded a high level of courage and endurance. "Don't give up the ship" took on poignant meaning for lightship crews. Regardless of the roughness of a storm or the threat by mountain-high waves, crew members had to remain with their vessel—that was their only hope of survival. Hurricanes posed the toughest of conditions for landlubbers; lightships were like toy boats in a great pond when hurricane-force winds and swells rushed upon them. George Putnam quoted Master Claudius Cecil Austin's personal account of riding out a 1933 hurricane on his light vessel stationed at Diamond Shoals:

> On the morning of [September] 15th the weather showed indication of a hurricane. At 8 a.m. wind forty and forty-five miles per hour, increasing, barometer falling. I got engine under way and began to work ahead slow. From noon to 4 p.m. wind east-northeast between fifty and sixty miles per hour, increasing, barometer falling. Seas getting rough and washing ship badly.
>
> At about 2 p.m. station buoy sighted for the last time as the weather was thick with rain and spray. I judge the ship began to drag anchor at about 4 p.m., wind increasing to about seventy miles per hour. I began to increase the speed of the engine from forty to sixty revolutions per minute. From 8 p.m. to midnight, wind east-northeast, between seventy and eight-five miles per hour, barometer falling. Seas were getting mountainous high and washing the ship terribly. Engine speed increased to ninety revolutions per minute.
>
> September 16th, between midnight and 1 a.m. ship went into breakers on southwest point of Outer Diamond Shoals (having dragged the fifty-five-hundred-pound anchor and twenty-four thousand pounds of chain the five miles from her station). Wind

The last Diamond Shoals lightship was the WLV 189, which served on station from 1946 until 1967. Evident below are the rough waters with which the ship had to contend, the result of the junction of the remnants of cold currents from the north and the warm Gulf Stream.

Lightship crews often compared their duty to imprisonment with only seasickness to break the tedium. Another observer referred to a lightship as a "tossing island" and said, "About the time a person gets accustomed to the pitching and plunging [the ship] begins to rear and roll."

about one hundred and twenty miles per hour. The first breaker which came aboard broke an air port in the pilot house which struck me (master) in the face and around the neck and on arm, cutting face and neck badly. This same breaker carried away one ventilator close to the pilot house. Mate S. F. Dowdy tried to get a stopper in the hole in the deck and was washed against a davit and broke some ribs. He was almost washed overboard. From 4 to 5 a.m. wind decreasing to about fifty miles per hour, barometer falling to 28.19 (lowest point).

We laid in the breakers from 12 midnight until 6:30 a.m., breakers coming aboard, breaking up everything on upper deck, washing boats, ventilators, awning stretchers away, bending awning stanchions inboard. Taking water in around umbrella of smokestack and through ventilators to such an extent that the water was rising at times above the fire-room floor with all pumps working, and every means we had to keep the water out of the ship. At 5:30 a.m. day began to break, so I could see the conditions outside. I could see an opening about south-southwest from the ship that looked like a chance to get away. Breakers coming over at intervals and I decided that it was the only chance out. I told the mate to get ready to slip the mooring, as we had to get out of that place, for when the wind comes from the west it would carry her into the breakers and finish her up. I slipped the mooring at 6:30 a.m. and got the ship outside the breakers, at about 7:15 a.m. being in the center of the hurricane. I had just got the breakers behind me when the wind struck from the west at about ninety miles per hour. I ran the ship southeast until I was sure I was all clear and then ran northeast thinking the hurricane would pass. I ran this course for a while and it did not get any better. I considered it was moving very slow (the barometer was rising fast) so I changed my course to south and ran this course until I ran out of the hurricane.

September 17th, 5 a.m. wind northwest, strong gale, but decreasing. At 6 a.m. I called the mate and told him to get the crew out and see if he could get the wireless antenna fixed up so that we could establish communication. (There had been no radio communication since Friday evening.) About 9 a.m. I got radio compass bearings which put the ship approximately sixty miles east-northeast from Cape Hatteras Lighthouse; at 4 p.m. radio bearings placed the ship about one hundred and ten miles east-southeast from Cape Henry. All the crew were at hand at all times and ready to do everything they could to help save the ship, both deck and engine force. During the storm one of the fusible plugs in the boiler blew. They let all steam from the boiler and opened up the furnace, went inside and took out the fusible plug that had blown and put in a new one, and closed the furnace and got steam on the boiler in the strength of the hurricane. I consider this a

The end of an era is captured in this photograph as the Diamond Shoals lightship heads for port, leaving the tower to flash its warning to ships. The oil rig–style tower was completed in 1967 as a manned station. It has since been automated. The tower's beacon can be seen as far away as seventeen miles.

brave deed, and M. W. Lewis and J. J. Krass, firemen, and A. D. Ameyette, seaman, are due all credit for accomplishing this job. I consider each and every man of the crew did all in his power, and through their bravery, energy, and willpower we brought the ship through the hurricane and safely into port. The vessel I consider a most excellent seaworthy ship to come through such a severe hurricane with such comparatively slight damage as was sustained; so much water came aboard that at times there was three feet of water in the engine-room bilges.

Austin received a letter of commendation from President Franklin D. Roosevelt after the ordeal, which was framed and placed aboard the lightship. In it the president said, "I am fully appreciative of the exceptional character of the services performed in saving this vessel, and in the protection of the shipping along the coast; and I wish you would convey to [the crew] my personal commendation for the manner in which they performed their dangerous duties during this storm."

A similar storm hit this same Diamond Shoals lightship in November 1934—and again it survived. Commissioner Putnam believed the success was due to improved lightship design, particularly in mooring chains. In his *Sentinel of the Coasts*, he wrote that the "breaking strength" in chains had doubled in the seven long decades lightships served at Diamond Shoals, and "even a 'West India' hurricane passing up the coast now seldom parts a lightship's mooring. In the great gales of September 1933 and November 1934, Diamond Shoals Lightship dragged her 5,500 pound mushroom anchor with 24,000 pounds of chain, for 5 miles in one storm and 3 and ½ miles in the other, but the mooring chain stood the tremendous strain and did not part."

From 1918 to 1967 a number of lightships stood defiant watch on Diamond Shoals, and a buoy marked the area during World War II. In 1967 Light Vessel 189 slipped its mooring and sailed away in farewell. Its services were no longer needed. Diamond Shoals Tower, a "Texas tower design" described by others as a "Gulf oil-rig structure," had taken over the lightship's duty of warning mariners away from the shoals.

Built for the U.S. Coast Guard, Diamond Shoals Tower was the first (and only) offshore lighthouse to be completed on Diamond Shoals. Four steel pilings driven into the sand twelve and a half miles south-southeast of Cape Point raise the square tower 125 feet above the water. Automated in 1977, its one-thousand-watt bulb flashes its warning from a solar-powered digitally controlled beacon. As long as its footing remains firm in the shifting sands off Cape Hatteras, this unmanned ghostly structure will continue the legacy of its predecessors in improving mariners' chances of safely navigating past the long-feared and highly respected Diamond Shoals.

THE CAPE HATTERAS BEACON LIGHT

Another small but rugged lighthouse that helped mariners in the Diamond Shoals area was the Cape Hatteras Beacon. Located about one and a half miles south of the main tower on the cape, the Hatteras Beacon was first operated in 1856. It stood on the edge of an area known as Cape Point and was exposed to the fury of southerly storms and the constant threat of erosion. The square wooden tower had an iron lantern, painted red, and was equipped with a rare sixth-order Fresnel lens that generated a fixed white light. The tower was only about twenty-five feet tall, but it was considered a giant by those who relied on the beacon.

For "coasting" vessels, fishermen, and casual boaters using the Diamond Slough (or Slue) Channel between the shoreline and the first shoals, the Hatteras Beacon was a welcome sight each evening when they returned from a rigorous day on the water. Its beam was an added comfort to these small craft as they tried to find their way through shrouds of fog or sheets of rain around the cape and into Pamlico Sound. The combination of the lighthouse and the beacon allowed captains to more accurately plot their position.

The beacon light at Cape Hatteras was first lit in 1856. Its primary duty was to guide ships through the sloughs between the shoals in front of the cape and assist local vessels in and out of the Pamlico Sound. Early reports describe the Hatteras beacon as painted red. Its sixth-order Fresnel lens generated a fixed white light that was visible for ten and a half miles. Although it might be considered "small," the Hatteras beacon was sufficiently important to be listed among the primary coastal lights and not with the smaller beacons and buoys.

In its half century of service, it was rebuilt in 1857 and 1883 and moved in 1890, according to the Light Lists of the Lighthouse Service. Responsibility for the beacon was delegated to the third assistant at the Cape Hatteras Light Station. That position was eliminated in 1906, about the same time the beacon disappeared from Lighthouse Service records. Miraculously it had survived the Civil War and the clashes between Confederate and Union soldiers wrestling for control of Hatteras Island. The beacon's Fresnel lens was reportedly lost during these engagements. It was temporarily lit by a steamer's lamp then refitted with a new lens.

The beacon stood as a silent sentinel while the 1870 lighthouse at Cape Hatteras was under construction and the former tower was demolished. The beacon was there when the new tower received its famous stripes in 1873. The Hatteras beacon was decommissioned in 1879 but recommissioned five years later in response to public demand. The isolated structure survived countless hurricanes, including the infamous San Ciriaco in 1899.

Several times over its years of existence, the Cape Hatteras Beacon was knocked over, righted, and relighted. One story was told about third assistant keeper Wesley Austin in his obituary July 13, 1941. He was credited with "the night that he fought a hurricane and sweeping breakers to gain a foothold on this old beacon—how, while applying a flame to the oil wick, the old beacon soon to be abandoned, gave a lurch and toppled over to a 45 degree angle. With a prayer on his lips, this man of great faith, clung to the leaning structure, lighted and adjusted the lamp so that its beam of light might warn mariners of the dangerous sand bar nearby. An unselfish prayer was his."

Many lights have come and gone since the first navigational light flickered across the barren sand of Cape Hatteras. Yet none possessed the reputation and distinctiveness of the famous black-and-white striped tower with the red-brick-and-granite foundation. From one century to the next, the lighthouse, a few supporting lightships, and an auxiliary beacon successfully addressed the navigational task for which they had been designed: Ships safely maneuvered through the waters off Hatteras Island.

7

THE THIRD LIGHTHOUSE

AUTOMATION AND THE END OF AN ERA

THROUGHOUT THE REMAINDER OF the nineteenth century and into the first decades of the twentieth, ships at sea had dependable navigational lights to chart their course around Diamond Shoals. By the end of the First World War, however, it was obvious that there was a problem of a different sort at the Cape Hatteras Lighthouse. In 1920 the ocean was less than one hundred yards away from the tower and advancing at an alarming rate. To stem the assault, crews placed wooden and sheet-steel jetties and sea walls on the beach in front of the tower, but the lighthouse was losing the battle. By 1931 storm-driven waves routinely washed around the base of the tower. A pair of hurricanes in 1933 forced the keepers' families to find safer ground as the sea washed through their dwellings. They would never return.

Keenly aware that the lighthouse at Hatteras might succumb to the ocean at any time, lighthouse officials decided it was time to abandon Stetson's 1870 tower and move the beacon to safer ground. In 1935 they selected a site on a small hill in the dense maritime forest west of the Cape Hatteras Lighthouse. There crews erected a 150-foot-tall skeletal steel tower. On top they placed a

In 1919 Myrtle was the first of the Jennette children to be born at the principal keeper's house at Cape Hatteras. The 1870 keepers house had been built of bricks left over from the venerable tower itself. "Mama was pregnant with me when she and Daddy first moved to the light station," Myrtle said recently. Eighteen months later her brother, Rany, was born. "Mama said people who didn't know us thought we were twins," she laughed.

Concerning her life at the light station, Myrtle recalled, "All I can say is that we had a wonderful life. We thought we were so isolated from the rest of the islanders. But we didn't know any different then. We had all the Casey and Quidley children to play with. My best friend was Myrtle Casey. People called her 'Big Myrtle' and me 'Little Myrtle.'" For toys and other necessities, she said that the family either shopped in Buxton or her parents ordered through the mail.

The lighthouse children, as all children will, got into mischief sometimes. "Rany could find all sorts of things to do. Did he tell you about the time he painted the red base of the lighthouse with tar? And Daddy made him wait for three days to find out what his punishment was. But Daddy didn't hurt him with the razor strap half as much as he hurt his feelings."

Myrtle's mother, Jenny Louanna Scarborough Jennette, was known as "Sudie" to everyone. "Mama was very reserved. She only saw good in people. And Daddy—he was respected. I never heard her or Daddy argue—no cross words between them.

"I remember," she continued, "the lighthouse tender coming in the sound from Baltimore and Daddy would go out [in a boat] to pick up the inspector. Sometimes he came unexpected, and I remember the funny feeling of seeing someone we considered a stranger. But the tender brought supplies and medicines. Everything you'd need.

"And I remember going up the stairs to the top of the lighthouse many, *many* times. In fact, Mama told me that after Rany was born and when she was busy with the three other children in the house, Daddy would carry me up the stairs with him to tend to the light. I can remember clearly seeing him draw back the linen curtains and light the lamp. And clean the lens . . . yes, and clean everything."

Myrtle Jennette and her brother, Rany, in 1939.

Myrtle was given chores around the lighthouse. "Now that I think back," she reminisced, "I didn't do half as much as I should have to help my mother. Oh, we took turns doing the dishes [for nine family members!] and helped around the house, but Mama and Daddy took care of most of the chores. Daddy took care of all the cows and pigs and chickens and horses. And we loved seafood."

Unaka Jennette, Myrtle's father, known as "Captain," held the highly prized job of principal keeper at the Cape Hatteras Light Station from 1919 until the station was closed in 1936. "We had two bad storms in 1933, I believe it was," Myrtle remembered. "And Daddy moved us to a house in the neighborhood. We were all very sad when the station closed in 1936. And you know, it is still home to me. Always will be."

Part of the relocation of the lighthouse is designed to furnish both keepers homes as interpretive exhibits for visitors. There may yet come a day when Myrtle can walk back into her childhood home and see her doll on the Victorian sofa in the living room, the Victrola she listened to many nights, and the piano in the front living room where Mother played sing-alongs for family and friends.

90,000-candlepower flashing white electric light. The beacon was a respectable 166 feet above sea level and could be seen nineteen miles at sea. The steel tower, referred to at the time as "the third Cape Hatteras light" and "the Buxton light," was completed and ready for service by May 1936.

On the night of May 13, 1936, engineers activated the new light tower. As its rotating light spun over the darkening Hatteras Island landscape, it illuminated the darkened tower 1,800 yards to its east. For the first time in sixty-six years, Stetson's lighthouse was dark.

Although the U.S. Lighthouse Service had given up on the Cape Hatteras Lighthouse, administrators with the National Park Service had not. When the Lighthouse Service relinquished its claim on the 1870 tower, the secretary of the interior formally requested the lighthouse and the forty-four acres of land surrounding its base for inclusion into the National Park Service's proposed seashore for the Outer Banks.

For nearly a decade, support had been building for the seashore, which would be the first of its kind in the nation, both from local officials and from major metropolitan newspapers such as the *New York Times.* Planners brushed their hands across maps of the broad sweep of North Carolina's barrier islands stretching from Kill Devil Hills south to Ocracoke as they presented the proposal to committees and community meetings throughout the country.

National Park Service officials jumped at the chance to include the Cape Hatteras Lighthouse in the package. Although it would be another dozen years before the first paved roads began to connect the isolated villages of Hatteras Island, the planners were looking to the future.

"In the general development now in progress involving the North Carolina seacoast from Kill Devil Hill and Roanoke Island, southward beyond Cape Hatteras, there has arisen the possibility of securing, under the jurisdiction of this Service, what is perhaps the most historic lighthouse on the Atlantic coast, namely the Cape Hatteras Lighthouse," claimed a July 1936 park service memorandum. "The Bureau of Lighthouses, Department of Commerce, has declared the Cape Hatteras Lighthouse, with two parcels totaling 44 acres, surplus to the needs of the Lighthouse Service. The opportunity is therefore presented to secure this property without cost and to preserve it as part of the general development of the North Carolina seacoast . . . as well as with the general recreational development. With Derby Wharf National Historic Site in Massachusetts and the Cabrillo National Monument on a famous Pacific Coast point in California, the Cape Hatteras Lighthouse will make

Already looking the part of a national landmark, the Cape Hatteras Lighthouse towers above every other structure on the surrounding sands in this 1905 photograph. In 1933, Frank Stick, an Outer Banks developer, preservationist, and artist, advocated a national park for the region. He wrote a series of newspaper articles calling for a coastal park in the state. Congressman Lindsay Warren brought the matter to Congress, and in 1937 federal legislation provided funding for the park and underwrote the work of the Civilian Conservation Corps in stabilizing the beaches of the Outer Banks.

three areas under this Department, permanently preserving key sites and structures intimately associated with the history of maritime America."

The next month, on August 4, 1936, the Department of the Interior formally requested the title to the lighthouse and its grounds. On August 31, Wayne C. Taylor, acting secretary of the treasury, notified the secretary of the interior that the National Park Service would receive the property.

As the property transfer was finalized in Washington, D.C., more immediate attention was being paid to the lighthouse by the members of the Civilian Conservation Corps (CCC). Working from a camp south of the Cape Hatteras light, CCC members built two courses of protective dune lines in front of the lighthouse and along the length of Hatteras Island. In between and on top of the dune lines they planted hundreds of thousands of beach grass plants to help anchor the new dunes against the near-constant winds of the Outer Banks.

In 1936, with the new double lines of dunes in front of the light and the remains of the 1920s wooden and steel groins still in place under the breakers, something amazing began to occur: The ocean slowly withdrew from the base of the light. The gradual retreat continued until the surf was more than six hundred feet to the east.

With a sturdy set of dunes and fresh claim to the property, park service officials now turned their attention to Stetson's tower and the keepers quarters. Although the station had been decommissioned less than a year before, a 1937 inspection showed them to be in need of substantial maintenance.

During the summer of 1937, park service staff and CCC members worked to repair the lighthouse and the keepers quarters. In the tower, they painted the interior walls, metal, and woodwork, repaired or replaced windows and glass, and built shutters to protect the windows. Work was equally comprehensive at the two keepers dwellings, each structure receiving a thorough face-lift inside and out. By the time the last paintbrush was cleaned and finishing touches were placed on the landscaping around the keepers quarters, the station looked reborn.

Interest in the proposed seashore grew, and soon development along the northern beaches of the Outer Banks blossomed into an array of beach cottages filled with eager, adventurous visitors. They soon began to look south, across Oregon Inlet, at the wild, untouched reaches of Hatteras Island. Fifty miles below the inlet, at the pronounced bend in the island where the banks begin to fall slowly back toward the west and the Carolina mainland, lay the Cape Hatteras Lighthouse. On August 17, 1937, Congress enacted legislation establishing the Cape Hatteras National Seashore Recreation Area thus making it official: The Outer Banks were open for business. It was only a matter of time before people came, park planners predicted.

"It is not much more difficult to build roads south of Oregon Inlet than it is to build them along the shore in Nags Head. The obstacles are about the same. True, the ferry charge at Oregon Inlet is now about $1.00; but a greater demand and a new ferry might cut this cost and lead to the exploitation of the fine beaches to the south," predicted Charles Porter, a park service field investigator at the time.

This 1905 photograph illustrates the starkness of the Hatteras light station. It would be another thirty years before the CCC erected the now-familiar dunes in front of the lighthouse, which would be to the left of the photograph. The ruins of the 1803 tower are visible to the right of the lighthouse.

"Should this development ever take place, few visitors could resist the temptation to ascend the lighthouse tower," Porter continued. "The view from the lantern gallery gives a magnificent sweep of the sea, the coast to the north, and the Cape of the south. Even now, before any museum has been installed, the ascension of the lighthouse tower and the examination of the lens is a thrilling educational experience never to be forgotten."

Porter pointed to the successful effort to repel the advancing ocean: "We may conclude that the historic old beacon has been saved and that it is now time to think of how we can secure the maximum educational value from this monument which epitomizes sixty-six years of vigilance and historic effort to save ships from the graveyard of the Atlantic."

At the top of the tower, the beautiful Fresnel lens still stood where Crosman had placed it on that late fall day in 1870. "The lens is a great barrel-shaped affair," Porter reported, "a veritable column of prisms and

bull's-eye lenses of optical glass set in bronze by Henry LePaute, Paris, France. The bull's-eye lenses are eleven inches in diameter and there are twenty-four of them. This great barrel-shaped complex of prisms and lenses revolves around the light.

"The lens is turned by a clock-like mechanism run by weights," he explained, marveling at the still-intact nineteenth-century machinery. "The works in this apparatus are of brass and hand-forged iron. The weights used in 1870 were round but eventually had a tendency to turn because long flat weights sliding on tracks have been substituted for the earlier ones."

With the support of Congress, the National Park Service, the CCC, and the increasing interest of the visiting public, it seemed the Cape Hatteras Lighthouse had been saved from an uncertain future. The ocean was again safely at bay, and the tower and dwellings were in fine shape. It appeared that all was well at Hatteras, but it would not remain so.

Three years after the lighthouse had been replaced by the skeletal tower at Cape Hatteras, World War II engulfed Europe. In preparing the United States for possible involvement in the world-wide struggle, the Lighthouse Service was merged with the U.S. Coast Guard in 1939, and the lives of the keepers and their families were forever changed. In retrospect, the steps taken in this merger

This late 1930s aerial view illustrates the first erosion control efforts made to protect this guardian of the Graveyard of the Atlantic. Visible in the upper right corner is the CCC camp. In other conservation efforts, laborers from eastern North Carolina made up many of the ranks of workers who built dunes, sand fences, and planted vegetation in an effort to rehabilitate and stabilize the beaches stretching along the Outer Banks.

were sound, but it could be argued that the Lighthouse Service was one of the first victims of World War II in America.

The 1939 merger of the Bureau of Lighthouses with the Coast Guard was orchestrated by President Franklin D. Roosevelt during his second reorganization plan. At the time, no one knew FDR's overall agenda or even if there was an overall plan. Like most domestic political decisions, the programs of the New Deal carried with them a measure of uncertainty. Generally speaking, they were steps to address immediate fears and had little regard for long-range effects. In this instance, the reorganization of the Lighthouse Service had severe ramifications for Cape Hatteras. The genesis of those problems, however, began almost twenty years prior to FDR's presidency.

From the moment George R. Putnam had stepped into the position as commissioner of lighthouses in 1912, his goal was to keep the Lighthouse Service on the ever-changing threshold of technology. Ultimately, however, the implementation of electronic controls, which Putnam advocated for the Lighthouse Service, led to the extinction of lighthouses as crucial navigational aids. Electrification, radio detection finding, and automated lighthouses gradually reduced the need for on-site supervision of the light stations. As early as 1927 traditional lighthouses were being replaced with automatic beacons.

In 1935 Putnam retired and his deputy, Harold Davis King, assumed the office of commissioner of lighthouses. In 1939 King led the service into the merger with the Coast Guard—or rather its absorption. The joining of the two services was not an uneventful process, however.

The annual reports of the Lighthouse Service for the first half of 1939 gave no indication of the end of the service or the imminent merger. Instead, the January bulletin initiated a series of five accolades for the service. In this first installment, Commissioner King praised and highlighted the strengths of the department's decentralized organization and its ideals of reliability, service, and progress in providing safeguards for life and property—the "watchwords" throughout the Lighthouse Service. At the same time, King addressed the field employees and engineers and suggested that they maintain a sense of humor and perspective on all matters relating to the service. Looking back, some have wondered if this was a hint of the plans to combine the two services and a suggestion that criticism of the move was not welcome.

The first five monthly bulletins of 1939 also noted that the Lighthouse Service administered twenty thousand navigational aids. Other articles offered retrospectives on the achievements of the service. In the February 1939 annual report, King possibly tipped his hand when he wrote: "Between the reefs of radicalism in any line of thought or action there is usually a conservative mid-channel course. . . . Between these extremes, the capacity to conceive new ideas, derived from a broad understanding of underlying principles and the following through to their practical application—In an individual, an industry, or a nation—guarantee achievement of progress and lasting success."

On May 9, 1939, Roosevelt's reorganization plan was announced. The news of the absorption of the Lighthouse Service by the Coast Guard was apparently a complete surprise to the lighthouse keepers. While rumors had been rampant among the ranks, until the announcement, many had nurtured the hope that it was not true. In the June 1939 Lighthouse Service bulletin, Commissioner King pointed out that the Coast Guard needed training in all the tasks and duties required to manage the light stations. In the same publication, it was announced that King, the deputy commissioner, and the chief engineer of the Lighthouse Service had each been appointed "assistant to the Commandant [of the Coast Guard], Russell Waesche."

For many within the lighthouse community the news was a blow to the integrity of the service. The Lighthouse Service had been formed in 1789, one year before the Coast Guard, and the department had always been praised for its leadership and efficiency.

King admitted in a May 17, 1939, letter to John Gaskill, the principal lighthouse keeper at Bodie Island, that most likely the military would "rule" in this merger:

> The ultimate authority in such matters will, of course, rest in the Treasury Department and upon recommendation of the Commandant of the Coast Guard rather than with this office since it appears quite within the realm of probability or at least possibility that the existence of the Lighthouse Service as a separate entity of the Government may cease when this Order takes effect.
>
> Please accept my best wishes for the future well-being of yourself and many other loyal employees of the Lighthouse Service with whom it has been my pleasure to serve during the best part of a life-time.

In June 1939 the merger became official. The light stations became Coast Guard bases, and some personnel, especially lightship engineers and engine room staff, served the needs of the Coast Guard well. Rumblings of distrust and doubt, however, echoed throughout the ranks of Lighthouse Service personnel. Difficult times lay ahead for the old lighthouse veterans.

Lighthouse employees had three choices: retire, remain civilian and retire under the Lighthouse Service retirement program

Although the Cape Hatteras Light Station might have been one of the most respected light stations in the country, it was still subject to inspection by the district inspector. In the 1920s Cape Hatteras was part of the Fifth Lighthouse District and under the scrutiny of Harold D. King. Hatteras's principal keeper, Unaka Jennette, prepared for these white-glove inspections much as an officer prepares his troops.

Such visitations left lasting impressions on the keepers' families. Jennette's two children, Rany and Myrtle, both remember the inspector's visits and knew that their father worked diligently to run a tight station with all shipshape for the inspections, planned or surprise.

Inspections were not always all work and terse exchanges between the district inspectors and the lighthouse keepers. There were chances for horseback rides to explore the settings and time to admire the magnificent lighthouse.

The lighthouse keepers' children were well dressed, meals were served by servants, and the good china and silver were spread on the table. While the inspectors and sometimes their family members were on station during such duty calls, the two families often took turns entertaining each other.

This photograph was taken during one of Harold King's inspections in the 1920s. It shows the fence around the base of the lighthouse, which kept livestock away, and the principal keepers quarters still in its natural brick color.

Inspectors traveled to the lighthouses under their charge aboard lighthouse tenders and were treated as high-ranking officers. Rany recalled going aboard the tenders—including the *Holly*, which he remembered as a sidewheeler—and exploring the engine rooms. The machinery inspired his dream of working as an engineer aboard such a vessel. Years later he realized that dream when he served with the navy during World War II.

King's children, Jack and Edith, were photographed (left) aboard the lighthouse tender *Holly.* Edith recalled, "My memory of Cape Hatteras is of swarms of mosquitoes eating me alive when we went ashore." After the inspection, King (right) enjoyed rides around the island on the ponies kept by the principal keeper, Unaka Jennette. King had a warm rapport with the men in his district from 1914 to 1929. That trust over the years led him to become deputy commissioner of lighthouses in 1929 and finally to serve as the last commissioner of lighthouses from 1935 to 1939.

The third Cape Hatteras Light-house was a 150-foot-tall skeletal tower. The tower (near right) was completed on September 18, 1935, but did not show its light until May 13, 1936. The electric beacon at the top of the tower (far right) superceded the Fresnel lens in the Stetson tower. For the first time in more than a century, the lighthouse at Cape Hatteras was dark.

(prepared on June 20, 1918, and approved by Congress for those affected by the merger through August 10, 1939), or enlist in the Coast Guard. Enlistment was allowed based on age, health, and length of service. Nevertheless, the transition was considered unfair by many lighthouse keepers.

In each lighthouse district, the district superintendent made recommendations regarding each individual who chose to enlist in the Coast Guard. Some superintendents protected their people and ensured that their experienced keepers received higher ratings. In many cases, however, uneven treatment began years of dissatisfaction because some men with just one light station to tend and fewer years of service were given the rank of chief, the highest enlisted rank in the Coast Guard. Others whose responsibilities included a light station, miles of navigational aids, rescue work, and excellent seamanship skills were granted only boatswain's mate, first class ratings. Furthermore, keepers who rated less than chief were asked to switch from their stately blue wool uniforms and don the white "monkey suits and cocked hats" of enlisted Coast Guard personnel.

These postings rankled more than a few lighthouse keepers and assistant keepers who, despite their civilian status with the Lighthouse Service, had been treated with a respect equal to that accorded commissioned officers in the Coast Guard. For example, Unaka Jennette, principal keeper at Cape Hatteras, had been called "Capt'n 'Naka" by all who knew and respected him.

About half of the Lighthouse Service force retired voluntarily. Others chose to retire after they had volunteered to enlist in the Coast Guard and were told that they might be transferred to other areas.

Hatteras Keeper Jennette became a civilian employee of the Coast Guard, but he was transferred from the skeletal tower at Hatteras to the remote Roanoke Marshes Lighthouse, which was a position hardly fitting a respected principal keeper with twenty years' experience. Young coastguardsmen took over at Hatteras and operated the electric beacon while others manned the darkened spiral-painted Hatteras tower to watch for the shadows of German U-boats in the nearby waters.

"It was a clash of cultures," Coast Guard historian Robert Browning said. "Homesteading keepers," as they were called among the Coast Guard youngsters, versus the "military regimen" that was thought to be superior. "And I'll tell you where the Lighthouse Service personnel got shorted," Browning offered. "It was in the positions they were offered and the pay and benefits they received, or better put, didn't receive."

The era of manned light stations was gone, and the light towers became either landmarks for sightseers or lookout posts. Records indicate that three hundred thousand people visited light stations in 1938. When the light stations were electrified and the two coastal services were consolidated, a way of life passed into history. No more would the needed work and repairs at a light station be done by just one or two light keepers, many with families who worked alongside them.

August 7, 1939, was designated as Lighthouse Week. Accolades from the White House rained down on the lighthouse community, applauding the "splendid work of the Lighthouse Service for 150 years in the safeguarding of life and property upon the sea." At the same time, Coast Guard Day was observed at the New York World's Fair. It was the first time that the Lighthouse Service had not been represented at a major exhibition in this country. Usually the service had been a center of attention with its magnificent Fresnel lens display, whistling buoys, and fog horns.

A final farewell was bid in a celebration of the 150th anniversary of the Lighthouse Service. Well attended by dignitaries, a celebration commemorating the history of the service was hosted by the Coast Guard commandant Russell Waesche at the 1791 Cape Henry Lighthouse, the first lighthouse contracted for construction by the federal government.

Great Britain and France declared war on Germany in September 1939 in response to the German invasion of Poland. At that time the most the United States could do was depend upon the Coast Guard to protect the coastline. President Franklin D. Roosevelt declared a 250-mile neutral zone off the coast and decided to strengthen the Coast Guard in every way possible. Merging the Lighthouse Service into the Coast Guard was part of this plan.

Principal keeper Unaka Jennette, the last keeper at Cape Hatteras, posed for *National Geographic* photographer Clifton Adams in 1933.

In September 1939, following the invasion of Poland and other ominous news from Europe, President Roosevelt issued an executive order preparing for an unnamed emergency and calling for increases in enlisted personnel throughout the military services, including the Coast Guard but exclusive of lighthouse crews. With the thunder of warfare echoing across the Atlantic, Roosevelt was anxious to plot a careful course should America be drawn into the war.

Two decades earlier, during World War I, German submarines had darkened the U.S. East Coast, interrupting shipping, wreaking havoc, and destroying the tanker *Mirlo* and the Diamond Shoals lightship. By strengthening the Coast Guard, Roosevelt had taken another step in preparing the country for a possible world war.

Within months the United States became involved in the clash with Germany through the lend-lease program with Britain and the Soviet Union. Twenty-seven months later, shortly after the Japanese attack on the American naval base at Pearl Harbor, U-boats took up positions along the East Coast of the United States. Systematically hunting for British and American petroleum tankers—the lifeline for the Allied war effort in Europe—German submarine commanders favored the waters off Cape Hatteras and described it as their "favorite killing field."

8

FROM DARKNESS TO LIGHT

THE WAR AND THE RESTORATION

IN JANUARY 1942, AS Kapitanleutnant Reinhard Hardegen gazed upon the bright lights of the U.S. coast through the periscope of U-123, he announced, "I have a feeling the Americans are going to be very surprised." As the group commander of a small fleet of six U-boats dispatched to disrupt American shipping immediately after the Japanese attack at Pearl Harbor, Hardegen wasted no time in sending the Panamanian tanker *Norness* to the bottom of the sea near the Rhode Island coastline.

During the next six months, U-boat captains exacted a terrible toll on the coastal shipping that was vital to the domestic economy of the United States and desperate to the Allied war effort in Europe. The German navy called the exercise *Paukenschlag,* meaning "Drumbeat," because the Nazi high command wanted the impact of these actions to reverberate across the United States and the rest of the world like the tremendous crash of a kettledrum. The operation had other names as well, specifically, "The Great American Turkey Shoot" and "The Second Happy Time." The hapless sailors whose ships plied the narrow shipping lanes along the Outer Banks knew it simply as "Torpedo Junction."

The U-boats sank more than eighty ships during a six-month period in 1942. Twenty-nine of those were off the North Carolina coast. Outer Banks residents still remember the bright flashes of light and muffled explosions in the eastern sky when the submarines took their deadly toll. Evidence of the action—wreckage, oil slicks, bodies, and debris—was scattered all over the beaches. Rumors claimed that spies were being landed everywhere.

It was not the first time the U-boats had come calling. A quarter century before, in the closing days of World War I, German submarines had prowled the American coast. Between April and November 1918, seven U-boats operating in U.S. coastal waters sank twenty-four commercial ships and seventy-six small schooners and fishing trawlers, including the Diamond Shoals lightship. The losses were absorbed into the larger news of the battles raging across the European countryside. While the surfmen of the life-saving service were busy rescuing survivors, the eyes of the nation were elsewhere. The losses during the early part of 1942, however, were a different matter altogether.

The U-boat attacks of 1918 and 1942 focused along the Outer Banks for two reasons. First, ships still had to negotiate the narrow passage between the Gulf Stream and Diamond Shoals. The concentration of ships rounding Cape Hatteras offered a seemingly endless number of targets. Second, by avoiding the dangers of Diamond Shoals, the ships were in deep water, a perfect environment for submarines. U-boat captains could rest underwater by day and surface at night to hunt, confident that a string of ships would pass along a predictable route each evening.

American military planners did little to help the merchantmen. During World War II in particular, no blackouts were enforced for the U.S. coast as had been done throughout England and Europe. Instead, acceding in part to pressure from coastal business owners who did not want to "inconvenience" tourists, officials ordered "dimouts" or partial blackouts designed to reduce the likelihood of silhouetting ships as they passed brightly illuminated towns, cities, and highways, giving submariners a clear target for their torpedoes. As part of this dimout policy, the 1936 Hatteras light tower was reduced from 80,000 candlepower to 12,000 candlepower in July 1942 and 5,600 candlepower in August 1942.

Dimouts, however, did little to reduce the rising number of ship losses during the first six months of the U-boat attacks. The glow from major U.S. cities was visible far out to sea. The blaze of light from New York City illuminated everything as far as twenty-five miles off the coast. Miami's lights were visible at thirty miles. The lights of Key West silhouetted ships thirty-five miles away. It

At 9 A.M. on March 26, 1942, the first torpedo from U-71 struck the *Dixie Arrow* amidships. The ship was carrying close to one hundred thousand barrels of crude oil, and it burst into flames. March 1942 was one of the worst months of the war for shipping along the Outer Banks. German submarines averaged sinking at least a ship a day, threatening the petroleum lifeline for industries in the North and also slowing down the flow of war materials to England during the early months of World War II.

would take more than a reduction in candlepower to repel the attacking submarines.

Nine ships went down off the North Carolina coast in January 1942, followed by another eight in February. By March a ship was lost almost every day. A military log at the time called the Carolina coast "the most dangerous area for merchant shipping in the entire world." U.S. officials realized they had to do something. The loss of ships, cargoes, and crews was threatening to stall the American economy and the Allied war effort.

Finally, in April 1942, the Americans collaborated with the British to assemble a fleet of twenty-four British antisubmarine trawlers to battle the U-boats. By the middle of May, a convoy system had been implemented, daily providing destroyer escorts for groups of ships sailing from Key West to Cape May. On the section of the trip between Cape Lookout and Chesapeake Bay, departures were timed to ensure passage around Cape Hatteras during daylight hours, a time when submarines shrank away from the powerful escort ships and prowling reconnaissance planes.

The efforts began to pay off almost immediately. Only eight ships were sunk in April, and that number dropped to three in May. More importantly, the combination of British antisubmarine trawlers and better preparations on the part of the Americans resulted in the first losses for the Germans. In April the destroyer *Roper* sank U-85 south of Wimble Shoals and the Hatteras Island community of Salvo. A month later the Coast Guard cutter *Icarus* sank U-352 off Cape Hatteras.

The tide had finally turned in favor of the Allies. In July, the German command ordered the remaining U-boats operating in U.S. waters to return to the mid-Atlantic, where they joined other submarines to prey on the convoys of men and materiel bound for the European theater. The U-boats were gone, but the damage they had done remained. The names of those lost at Torpedo Junction were added to the hundreds who had gone before them into the Graveyard of the Atlantic.

The Cape Hatteras Lighthouse had witnessed the sinking of more ships off its waters than the total number of ships lost at Pearl Harbor. During the month of March 1942, an average of at least one ship a day spread its load of oil on the sands of Diamond Shoals and Cape Hatteras.

Yet when the war ended so did the dreams of many Lighthouse Service personnel who had enlisted with the promise of better rank and pay after the war. A surplus of boatswain's first mates dashed all hopes of promotion, especially for the aging population of former Lighthouse Service employees. Many more retired, and the legacy of the Lighthouse Service dimmed more with each passing year.

After assuming the responsibility for hundreds of light stations in 1939, the Coast Guard found the rising costs of maintenance formidable. In a move to mend fences with lighthouse families and return some of the Lighthouse Service's history back to the public, the Coast Guard named some of its vessels after several women

This series of photographs reveals some of the restoration work begun in the lighthouse in 1991. In the image to the left, the metal brackets used as guides for the weights that turned the light can be seen. The interlocking stairwell can be seen in detail in the center photograph. The chariot wheels of the rotating Fresnel lens can be seen in the image to the far right.

who had served as lighthouse keepers, such as the *Abbie Burgess,* the *Ida Lewis,* and the *Katherine Walker.* In the following years, the Coast Guard began to relinquish ownership of dozens of former lighthouse towers to nonprofit groups for restoration and visitation. Light stations became one of the number-one destinations for families on vacation.

Regular reports by Coast Guard inspectors showed the Cape Hatteras Lighthouse to be in fine shape. In fact, it was in such good shape, with the ocean still a safe distance to the east, that one of the inspectors, Lt. Cmdr. F. I. Phippany, began to press for the reestablishment of the Hatteras light.

In September 1943 he raised the issue with his superiors: "In the course of travel to Cape Hatteras, [I] took the opportunity to inspect the old brick lighthouse at Cape Hatteras. It is in an excellent state of preservation. The lens, lens chariot, and clockwork could be put in use in a short time by cleaning and oiling. While a number of lantern panes are cracked, the lantern is otherwise in good shape. The wiring from the lens to the base of the tower appears O.K.—It is suggested that consideration be given to the exhibition of the Cape Hatteras light from the tower rather than the steel tower located back in Buxton Woods. It would be much more accessible to the new Cape Hatteras Coast Guard Station."

Apparently Phippany received no response to his suggestion. A little more than a year later, in October 1944, he again contacted his superiors, this time with a much different report:

> We inspected the old Hatteras Light on this trip. I inspected this tower about 13 months ago and on return to Headquarters recommended consideration be given to re-establishment of the Cape Hatteras Light in the old tower.
>
> That recommendation is renewed for the following reasons:
>
> (a) The shoreline is moving further away from the tower. The recent severe hurricanes have not changed the tendency of the beach to move out at Cape Hatteras.
>
> (b) Although the National Park Service has evidently made some of the repairs on the tower including a good paint job inside and out, it is not locked, nor has it been locked for some months if we may believe local gossip, and considerable vandalism is occurring particularly to the lantern and lens. The lens, a beautiful example of a first order 24 panel symmetrical fresnel lens has been permanently ruined by the removal of practically two complete flash panels and a start has been made on a third flash panel.
>
> (c) There is no more excellent land mark than this tower and the light should be exhibited from the same point.

(d) It is only about one mile from the Lifeboat Station and thus convenient for maintenance by Coast Guard personnel.

I consider it a pity to continue to fail to utilize this splendid tower as a lighted aid to navigation.

Reminders from World War II can still be found and explored on the beaches at Hatteras. This wreck of an LST (landing ship tank) was photographed inside and out in 1962, but it is now under water, claimed by the changing shoreline.

Phippany's superiors agreed with his recommendation, but they were still unsure that the efforts to hold back the ocean would continue to be successful. They suggested keeping the beacon on the steel tower "for a period of two or three years in order to better support the conclusion that the beach is no longer subject to excessive erosion. In the meantime, the old tower could be properly cared for thus preventing undue deterioration and should conditions finally suggest that the old tower be relighted, steps could be taken to effect the change probably with greater facility and at less cost than the present time."

Unfortunately, Phippany's superiors had missed a key element of his report. Vandals were attacking the lighthouse, stealing sections of the beautiful lens and breaking whatever they could not carry home as souvenirs. For another two years, little would be done to arrest the destruction. By the time any official action was implemented it was too late. The Fresnel lens, the wonderfully complex heart of the Cape Hatteras Lighthouse, had been destroyed.

In November 1946, Horace Dough, the custodian for Kill Devil Hill National Memorial and the man responsible for the upkeep of the historic structures on Hatteras Island, including the lighthouse, made a grim discovery.

> On a recent inspection trip of the Cape Hatteras Lighthouse property I found the lighthouse had been broken open by vandals and many of the window panes broken out. I also found that most of the heavy glass prisms that form the powerful lens for the light had been removed from about twenty-eight panels in the lens. . . .
>
> I noted that the heavy door lock on the steel entrance door had been torn off and the Coast Guard had refastened the door with a heavy iron chain and the doors had been broken open again by prying the bolts that held the heavy chain out of the steel doors.

Dough placed responsibility for the vandalism squarely at the feet of the Coast Guard.

> Since the Cape Hatteras Lighthouse was turned over to the Coast Guard in January, 1942, in order that they might establish a coastal look out station in the tower thereof—this office has never received any notice that the Coast Guard had turned it back over to the National Park Service—we assumed that it was still under the protection of the Coast Guard.
>
> If the Coast Guard has not relinquished their permit to use the lighthouse it seems to me that they might be willing to return it to our custody in as good condition (natural wear and tear accepted [*sic*]) as it was when we turned it over to them and in the event it has been officially returned to our custody perhaps they would be willing to give us a hand in restoring the damage.

Dough's reports set off a chain of events that eventually reached the upper levels of both the National Park Service and the U.S. Coast Guard.

A subsequent inspection revealed the extent of the damages:

> Subject lighthouse has been inspected and the following deficiencies noted.
>
> (a) Window panes in outside frame at top broken
>
> (b) Rail on outside at top badly rusted. One bottom section of rail missing.

(c) Lens on inside frame that protects main light is a total distruction [*sic*].

(d) Light missing and light stand is badly damaged.

(e) Both top decks badly rusted.

(f) All doors, windows, rails and lockers need replacing.

(g) Large crack from top deck visible.

(h) Fence around lighthouse total destruction.

(i) Lighthouse needs painting inside and out and all iron work needs chipping and painting.

(j) Oil house in need of all windows and doors, frames broken.

Coast Guard officials attempted to put the best face on the issue, saying they cared for the lighthouse as well as they could during a time of war, but that the Coast Guard had ceased to use the lighthouse property "sometime before the cessation of hostilities." Postwar personnel cutbacks had then left only a small crew at the lifeboat station near the lighthouse.

"During the war, while personnel were available, a careful watch was kept on the Lighthouse property. Since personnel were no longer available for watch on the property, it has been under the surveillance of the Cape Hatteras Life-boat Station; however, this simply includes a watch from the Lookout Tower at the Station proper and a periodic inspection of the property. I understand such a watch as this was effected even during peace time before the Coast Guard reoccupied the property in 1942," explained Coast Guard Admiral Shanley

After jurisdiction passed to the U.S. Coast Guard, Cape Hatteras was the scene of numerous Coast Guard Day celebrations. The event gave visitors a chance to see lifesaving drills performed, which included surf boat demonstrations. Here the crew from the Oregon Inlet lifesaving station prepares to launch its boat. The boat from Chicamacomico is in the background. Most likely the photograph comes from the 1940s or early 1950s.

to Thomas J. Allen, regional director of the park service in Richmond in a January 1947 letter.

Incredibly, Shanley attempted to explain away the vandalism as inevitable, even as he agreed to provide funding for at least some of the repairs: "This, of course, was simply a matter of cooperation with your Department; thus it is believed that the vandalism, as noted in your letter of December 4, 1946, would have occurred anyway. However, it has been a cause of distress to the Coast Guard to have this vandalism occur, and we are willing to effect such repairs to the property as can be accomplished with personnel and money available to us at this time. It must be pointed out, however, that we have no appropriation to cover any extensive amount of repairs."

Finally, Shanley agreed to provide better security at the lighthouse: "We have notified the Officer-in-Charge of the Cape Hatteras Lifeboat Station to take extra precautions, with personnel available, to prevent recurrence of any further vandalism and also to ascertain, if possible, the person or persons responsible for the vandalism."

Before long, local newspapers picked up the fight, accusing the park service, not the Coast Guard, of allowing the Cape Hatteras Lighthouse to fall into disrepair. The criticism stung park service officials who had already spent months coaxing even a minor level of cooperation from Coast Guard brass. At first glance, however, it is easy to understand the confusion. Although the Coast Guard had been responsible for the lighthouse during the war, their permit had expired in August 1947. The lighthouse was again park service property.

Throughout the remainder of 1947, park service and Coast Guard officials batted the issue of responsibility back and forth. Although increased security and surveillance seemed to have arrested any more significant vandalism, the damage had been done. Worse, the broken windows and doors were letting the fierce weather of the island gain ground on the tower. Rust and decay were beginning to take their toll.

Despite continued pressure by local park service staff and the local papers, little was done to correct the situation at the lighthouse throughout the remainder of 1947 and the early part of 1948.

The Cape Hatteras Lighthouse stands as a giant flagpole for the signal flags greeting a host of visitors during a Coast Guard Day in the 1950s. Note the wide beach in front of the lighthouse. The jeep in the foreground would be under water today.

A June trip to the light by Elbert Cox, the park service's regional director, summed up the damage:

> I climbed to the top of the tower very hurriedly during my trip to Hatteras in early May. I did not have the opportunity to make a thorough investigation, but I am sure that much more damage has been done to the old light and machinery than you realize. All of the prisms, except one, in the vertical panels or sections of the light have been broken or are gone. The larger prisms at the top and base portions of the light were apparently too strong for the tools at hand so remain in place, although the fine edges are badly chipped and scarred. I could see little or nothing in the way of machinery or parts which operated the old light.

Four months later Arthur Perkins, a park service planner, was more succinct: "It is, in fact, a disgrace. It appears the condition of the tower is a sore subject locally and with very good reason, even though it may not be just to attribute the fault to this Service."

Finally, in November 1948, the Coast Guard agreed to meet with the park service to assess the damage to the lighthouse and to see what was necessary to make repairs. The Coast Guard showed renewed interest in the lighthouse and began taking the first steps toward reestablishing the tower as a navigational aid.

After enumerating the long lists of deficiencies found at the light station, Coast Guard officials agreed to perform the necessary repairs. They also entered into an agreement specifying the upkeep of the lighthouse and the transfer of the remaining parts of the Fresnel lens to Horace Dough at Kill Devil Hill National Memorial for safekeeping. They agreed to try to find a replacement for the destroyed lens but apparently did little to follow through on the promise.

Repairs were made in early 1949, with the tower again receiving fresh coats of paint inside and out, the windows and frames put back in order, other necessary work attended to, and a six-foot-high chainlink fence placed around the lighthouse and oil house to protect the property from any future vandalism.

The remaining pieces of the lens were removed, packaged, and shipped to Kill Devil Hill where Dough received them. In place of the old lens, Coast Guard workers installed a new thirty-six-inch rotating duplex beacon. The electric light was powered by commercial current from the Buxton power station, with a backup generator in the oil house at the base of the tower.

On January 23, 1950, the change occurred. Eighty years after its completion, Stetson's tower, modernized with an electric light, was again flashing its warning across the sea.

PART 3

NATURE'S WAY

9

THE
ENCROACHING TIDE

SEVENTY YEARS OF FUTILITY

Come forward into the light of things,
Let Nature be your teacher.
                    WILLIAM WORDSWORTH, 1798

THE ISLAND CHAIN KNOWN as the Outer Banks is a child of the sea. Stretching for 150 miles in a thin ribbon from the Virginia border south to Cape Lookout, the narrow, low-slung islands form a breakwater for the North Carolina mainland that lies across the broad, flat, blue waters of Pamlico Sound.

Coastal experts warn that the barrier islands are like all other barrier islands—they move, driven by prevailing wind and water currents. The Outer Banks are a relatively young formation—less than ten thousand years old—and they are incredibly mobile. Since they were formed at the end of the last Ice Age, they have migrated as much as fifty miles from the edge of the Continental Shelf to their current location. And they're still moving.

When the Cape Hatteras Lighthouse was completed in 1870, the tower stood more than sixteen hundred feet from the ocean. There were no dunes in front of the lighthouse, in fact no dunes anywhere on most of the island. Table-flat stretches of sand stretched off to the water beyond. Engineers placed the tower at its current site because they believed it would be protected from the sea. For a while they were right, but over the years it became increasingly obvious that something was wrong. When the shore began to erode, some lighthouse officials considered abandoning the tower, and others claimed that the significance of the lighthouse mission justified erosion-control measures. In the seven decades since the lighthouse was decommissioned, more than $17 million have been spent to hold back the Atlantic and salvage the Hatteras beachfront. Nearly every engineering device known have been used to curb the loss of the protective beach in front of the lighthouse.

The following is a synopsis of the efforts to control erosion at the Cape Hatteras Light Station:

1920s . . .

During the 1920s islanders once enjoyed a beach so wide that they played baseball on a field between the tower and the ocean. By the mid-1920s, the ocean had advanced to within three hundred feet of the lighthouse. Local residents built dunes and planted native shrubs and beach grasses in an effort to stem the tide. The dunes and the sea walls that had been put in before them helped stop the advancing ocean, and for a time the sea actually retreated by as much as three hundred feet. By the early 1930s, however, the ocean was once again encroaching on the lighthouse.

The 1930s . . .

Despite more than a million-dollar expenditure in beach nourishment and protection along the Outer Banks during the mid-1930s, the

Free-range livestock roamed Hatteras Island until 1936 when penning laws were enacted to protect fledgling trees, shrubs, and grasses planted by the CCC to help anchor the newly constructed sand dunes.

ocean was lapping at the base of the lighthouse. After a pair of back-to-back hurricanes in 1933, seawater actually entered the base of the tower and forced the evacuation of the keepers' families. The families never returned.

Faced with the impending loss of an important maritime marker, in May 1936 federal lighthouse officials opted to extinguish the Cape Hatteras Lighthouse and erect a temporary beacon on a steel tower about a mile and a half inland on a wooded hill.

The Coast Guard absorbed the Lighthouse Service in 1939 and took possession of the Cape Hatteras Lighthouse.

The 1940s . . .

In 1948, the Coast Guard, caretaker of the lantern, and the National Park Service, now owners of the Cape Hatteras tower and surrounding land soon to become the Cape Hatteras National Seashore, began a joint project to restore the lighthouse.

More than a decade of abuse and neglect had taken its toll on the Hatteras lighthouse. Windowpanes were broken in the rusting lantern room, the Fresnel lens was damaged by souvenir hunters, and paint peeled from the tower's distinctive spiral bands.

The 1950s . . .

In January 1950, the lighthouse was again restored to full operation. Three years later, the Cape Hatteras National Seashore was officially opened, complete with a new two-lane highway stretching the length of Hatteras Island and reinforced by more than sixty miles of protective dunes. Public interest in the Hatteras lighthouse began to grow as the number of visitors to the landmark increased each year.

The 1960s . . .

The completion of the Bonner Bridge linking Hatteras Island with the mainland in 1963 turned the trickle of visitors into a torrent. Visitors flocked to the tower, eager to see the breathtaking view of the cape and Diamond Shoals.

Officials pumped more than three hundred thousand cubic yards of sand in front of the lighthouse in 1966, but it washed away almost immediately. In 1967 the park service used sandbags

At the beginning of World War II, Aycock Brown photographed the Hatteras light station. The white tower at the end of the road near the top of the image is a navy radio station in Buxton.

Because the tower is situated on the elbow-shaped area of Hatteras Island, it stands at the most eastern point on the East Coast between New York and Miami. This relatively close position to oceangoing vessels made the Outer Banks an ideal location for radio communication between ship and shore.

"Wireless telephones" were first tested here in 1901, broadcasting music from Hatteras to Roanoke Island. The first naval radio tower was erected on the lighthouse grounds in 1905. On the night of April 14, 1912, the Hatteras wireless operator picked up the distress signal from the *Titanic*.

These 1939 views of the beach from the top of the lighthouse show the foundation of the 1803 tower (near right) on the crest of a dune line and (facing page) several homes in Buxton, a radio tower, and a building that might have been a weather station.

to fortify the beach in front of the lighthouse. The ocean was also threatening a U.S. Navy base that had been built just north of the lighthouse. Alarmed by the encroaching waters, navy officials constructed three groins—sea walls placed perpendicular to the shoreline—to combat the erosion.

With the groins in place, sand accumulates on the "upstream" side while it erodes from the "downstream" side at an equal rate. The barriers did their job, but they caused another problem. In order to save the beach property from eroding immediately downstream from a groin, another groin must be built to accumulate the sand in that area and so on. In a chain reaction, the entire coastline downstream from the first groin must be protected with groins.

For that reason, North Carolina and other coastal states banned the use of groins and other types of sea walls in the mid-1970s. Exceptions would be allowed in cases like that of North Carolina's erosion-threatened Fort Fisher, an earthen historic site that could not be moved. State environmental laws and federal coastal laws affecting national seashores strictly disciplined the search for alternatives to relocation.

At Hatteras, the groins performed as expected. They trapped sand in front of the lighthouse, but they also interrupted the natural flow of sand. The beach on the downstream side, closest to the southeast corner of the lighthouse, began to erode. In time, the small indentation in the beach enlarged. The excavated area

became a weak spot in the lighthouse's lines of defense. Storm-driven waves overran the thin dune line and attacked the tower in a flanking movement.

The groins also created a much more serious problem. Under the breakers, the angle of the beach increased, and the waves pounded the beach head-on. This created a steeper drop-off on the beach as the ocean scoured the bottom of the beach itself. The steeper slope resulted in more erosion because the currents worked to restore the slope to a more natural angle, just as the walls of a trench dug in sand are sure to collapse.

Over time, the ocean scoured large amounts of sand from between the groins, requiring the pumping of millions of cubic yards of sand into the sagging spaces from other spots on the island. Although the sand built up the surface of the beach, the angle of the beach under the breakers continued to increase. As the surf line crept closer and closer to the base of the tower, park service engineers placed huge sandbags along the ocean side of its base, a last line of defense against the inexorable force.

The 1970s . . .

The ocean continued to advance on the lighthouse. As the situation grew more desperate, additional beach nourishment was attempted but failed. In 1975 the Atlantic was less than 200 feet from the base of the tower.

Part of the first annual Pirates Jamboree held at the Hatteras lighthouse in 1955 included a horseback ride past the tower. The event was sponsored by the Dare County Tourist Bureau and held the second week in April to attract and stimulate business. It lasted until 1964.

The early 1980s . . .

The original site of the 1803 tower was lost in a March blizzard in 1980. With the ocean only 150 feet away, state and federal officials decided to resolve the problem. A local group, the Outer Banks Preservation Association, was formed to generate and coordinate support for preservation efforts. It gained the backing of North Carolina Gov. James Hunt and U.S. Sen. Jesse Helms.

A newly created Save the Cape Hatteras Lighthouse Committee was formed by North Carolina entrepreneur and developer Hugh Morton, who gained the support of the North Carolina Travel Council, which spearheaded a statewide campaign to save the lighthouse. Schoolchildren donated nickels and dimes, and large corporations made sizable donations to the group.

By 1981 Morton's committee had a large sum of money but no new options. The funds were used to lengthen the steel groins near the lighthouse and pay for additional sandbags. The group also pressed for additional groins along the beach in front of the lighthouse, but it discovered new obstacles to that path. Coastal geologists, including Duke University's Orrin Pilkey Jr. and Robert Dolan Jr. from the University of Virginia, raised serious questions about the long-term effectiveness and impact of groins on ocean beaches.

In the meantime, Hatteras Island residents asked for more sand and additional groins to protect their property. The political environment, however, had changed. Long, hard-fought battles had gone into forming North Carolina's coastal laws to make groins and similar structures illegal.

In 1982 the National Park Service opted for a concrete perimeter, or sea wall, also known as a revetment, as the solution to the problems facing the lighthouse. The project was estimated to cost between $2 million and $3 million to initiate, with a final price tag estimated at approximately $5.5 million.

As the park service bureaucracy moved slowly toward construction of the revetment, laws restricting federal intervention against natural processes at a national seashore were enacted. Questions about the appropriateness of the revetment project were raised. Planners debated while the ocean continued to advance toward the tower.

The mid-1980s . . .

The Save the Lighthouse Committee funded the placement of artificial seaweed on the ocean floor in front of the lighthouse. At first these seemed to help, but not long afterward, the six-foot-long plastic fronds washed up on the beach following a storm.

At about the same time, David Fischetti, a North Carolina structural engineer, along with David Bush, then research associate for Duke University, and Barrett Wilson of the American Association of Cost Engineers began to question the decision to keep the ocean and lighthouse in place. They introduced the idea that the lighthouse could be moved to safety. The estimated price tag in the mid-1980s was $3 million to $5 million.

The move plan quickly gained support from marine geologists, construction engineers, and architects from across the country. In 1986 the multidisciplinary collection of researchers and scholars formed the Move the Lighthouse Committee, with Fischetti as president, to urge the park service to opt for relocation of the lighthouse.

The late 1980s . . .

In 1987, although funding and final plans were underway for the revetment, park service officials decided to commission a study by the National Academy of Sciences to review the lighthouse situation and recommend the best course of action. The following year, the NAS recommended the relocation of the lighthouse.

In 1989 plans for the revetment ended, and the park service announced it would follow the opinion of the NAS and begin plans

There were beach nourishment programs at the lighthouse in 1966, 1971, and 1973. The largest of these was the last one, between April and August 1973, and this photograph was likely taken during that time. These pipes were used to pump sand onto the beach in front of the lighthouse. Other erosion control methods used in the following years included repairing and extending the existing groins (sea walls), barriers made of huge sandbags, planting artificial seaweed, and even adding riprap from an old road.

Workers construct one of the first sea walls, or groins, in front of the lighthouse. The groins were supposed to catch the drifting sand from the Outer Banks current, but while that sand accumulated along the north side of the barrier, the sand along the south side was swept away.

for a move. Sealing the park service's commitment to relocating the lighthouse was data concerning the storm history in the Cape Hatteras vicinity. Officials determined that the risk of leaving the lighthouse where it was outweighed the risk of moving it to a safer distance from the ocean.

The Save the Lighthouse Committee donated additional sandbags, placed around the base of the tower, to buy time from the sea. Attention turned to the lighthouse itself.

The 1990s . . .

In 1990 the park service appropriated nearly $1 million to inspect and repair the lighthouse in preparation for the move. The company hired to do the work—International Chimney Corporation of Buffalo, New York—was renowned in this field. It studied every aspect of the lighthouse's construction and made the necessary repairs. Structural engineers declared the lighthouse fit for the move.

Although everything was in place for the move, the park service administration, under mounting pressure from the antimove camp, balked at the relocation idea.

Funds intended to begin the move process were redirected for emergency repairs to the three groins near the base of the lighthouse. More sandbags were placed in front of the tower.

In 1993 Hurricane Emily threatened to swamp the lighthouse. National seashore employees used everything they could, including

During its seventy years of operation, the 1803 Dearborn tower experienced severe wind erosion problems. It finally fell victim, however, to the surf during a rare late-winter blizzard in March 1980, which toppled the foundation onto the beach. Portions of the sand hill on which the first tower was built are visible in these photographs, but no trace of it remains today. This area is now under water.

This illustration is an artist's conception of the plan to maintain the lighthouse while the beach around it continues to erode. The plan was originally accepted by the National Park Service in 1982. Predictions that the lighthouse's foundation might not survive the loss of the fresh water table influenced the park service's decision to relocate the lighthouse.

riprap from an old service road near the tower, to hold back the waves. Their effort were successful, but the degree of risk to the lighthouse only increased. The beach on the south side of the tower continued to erode.

In 1995 Russell Berry, then NPS superintendent, requested a temporary fourth groin as the first part of a three-step plan to buy time until sufficient funds could be collected to finance the move. The fourth groin would be removed once the lighthouse had been relocated. The North Carolina Natural Resources Commission, wary of weakening state coastal laws, denied the request in 1996. When news broke of the state's preliminary refusal to allow the groin, the *Outer Banks Sentinel*—a local newspaper, the Outer Banks Lighthouse Society, and Cape Hatteras National Seashore officials pushed the issue to the forefront. State elected officials gradually signed on to support relocation.

The North Carolina Senate president pro tempore, Marc Basnight, became instrumental in crystallizing initial support for the move, estimated at $12 million. Basnight called for a team of North Carolina State University engineering and environmental professors to form an ad hoc committee to study the conclusions of the ten-year-old NAS study. The group issued a unanimous decision confirming the findings of the NAS study: If the lighthouse was to be saved for future generations, it should be moved. The committee also announced that the tower was sound and able to withstand the rigors of a move.

Erosion was a problem not only for the lighthouse, in the distance and to the left of this photograph, but also for Highway 12, the only paved road linking the northern and southern ends of Hatteras Island, marked by the telephone poles on the other side of these huge sandbags. Some sections of the highway have already been rebuilt farther away from the shore, toward the soundside of the island. The sandbags were placed here to absorb the impact of potentially damaging waves churned up by an approaching storm.

Basnight spoke with President Bill Clinton during the president's visit to Raleigh in 1997 and asked for his support in moving the lighthouse. Clinton agreed, appointing his chief of staff, Erskine Bowles, to head White House efforts.

U.S. Sen. Lauch Faircloth, with his chief legal aide Sean Callinicos keeping the senator apprised of the situation, became a strong supporter of the relocation project. Faircloth sought and received $2 million in the 1998 federal budget to allow the park service to plan and prepare for the move. The breakers were less than 130 feet away from the lighthouse.

"The lighthouse has become an ideological lightning rod," Callinicos remarked. "By the time [the debates] are over, the lighthouse could be a pile of bricks. Then wouldn't we look foolish? Everybody is concerned that if this topples, North Carolina will look idiotic, a state that can't protect its heritage."

For the first time the financial situation favored the relocation of the Cape Hatteras Lighthouse. The park service committed to the move, public officials favored it, environmentalists advocated it, the lighthouse community applauded it, the budget supported it, and the ocean demanded it.

1998 . . .

On October 16, 1998, Senator Faircloth announced that he had been successful in securing funds from Congress to move the Cape Hatteras Lighthouse. Finally, the stage was set to move the

After Hurricane Gordon struck the island in 1994, the dune line was severely shortened and the groins required extensive repairs. Sandbags were used to temporarily protect the shoreline from further erosion.

On the last day the lighthouse was open in 1998, before preparations were begun for the move, a young visitor enjoys the view. The proximity of the tower to the sea renders the view from the catwalk more like the view from a ship's deck.

nation's tallest brick lighthouse a distance of twenty-nine hundred feet to safety.

When the lighthouse is placed on its new site in July 1999, it will be about sixteen hundred feet from the ocean, the same distance to the sea as when Stetson's lighthouse was completed in 1870. Scientists say the new spot will ensure the lighthouse's continued survival for the next century.

In an interview in 1997, Cullen Chambers, restoration expert and site manager at Tybee Island Light Station near Savannah, Georgia, observed: "It was the policy of the United States Lighthouse Service to move its lighthouses out of harm's way whenever possible. Dozens have been moved since the service's beginning. Had technology been available, the great Cape Hatteras Lighthouse would have been moved long ago. Today, we have that technology and we must not lose this lighthouse. Retreating from the ocean is not a sign of weakness, but of *reason*."

10

Juggling a Stack of Bricks

Moving into the Future

Whoever wins the battle of ideas over what to do with the
Cape Hatteras Light will . . . set the tone for our response
on a national scale to the problem of retreating shores.
WASHINGTON POST, JANUARY 11, 1987

Erosion has threatened the Cape Hatteras Lighthouse from the beginning, ever since the first tower was constructed on the island. It has been a constant battle. The most persistent element in this contest has been the sea, sometimes creeping, sometimes charging, but always encroaching on the light station. Each wave has been a bit stronger, a bit closer, and a bit more determined to break through any line of defense. Most recently, the lighthouse has become a point of contention between two opposing camps, both of which has as its goal to preserve and protect it for the long term.

One camp wanted the lighthouse to remain in its original position, protected by sea walls and sand replenishment as the primary methods of stabilizing the beach near the tower. This group included county officials, some residents of Buxton, private property owners near the lighthouse, and the Save Cape Hatteras Committee. The second camp, made up of lighthouse preservationists, scientists, environmentalists, and the National Park Service, would prefer that the National Historic Landmark be moved away from the vulnerable edge of the Atlantic in compliance with state and federal coastal laws that prohibit any effort at hardening the coastline.

101

The first camp has waged a valiant but losing effort since the 1920s. In small private, local groups, and later with the backing of the Civilian Conservation Corps and the National Park Service, they battled the ocean with sea walls, sandbags, beach nourishment, and protective dunes. More than $17 million has been invested in these projects, but despite these best efforts, the ocean has continued to advance.

Park service officials have struggled to decide how best to preserve the lighthouse. An initial plan to construct a concrete revetment, or perimeter wall, around the base of the lighthouse, which would have allowed the tower to become an island as the ocean continued its advance, was scrapped in favor of relocation.

Over the last decade the disagreement between the residents of Hatteras Island, who opposed moving the lighthouse, and the supporters of the move turned bitter and attracted the eyes and ears of Congress. Finally a decision was made to move the lighthouse with the federal government appropriating roughly $12 million for the project.

International Chimney Incorporated (ICC) was chosen to do the job and drew up relocation plans and began preparation work in December1998. Expert House Movers, comprised of three generations of move specialists in the Matyiko family, worked with ICC to accomplish the relocation. Joining these experienced lighthouse movers were architects, surveyors, structural engineers, and experts in law and engineering.

In 1963, when this photograph was taken, the Cape Hatteras Lighthouse was much farther back from the ocean than it is today. The sea oats in the foreground are on a dune between the light and the breakers.

This view of the lighthouse, looking south, shows the accelerated erosion on the southern, downdrift side of the shoreline caused by the groins erected to trap sand and protect the beach and the naval installation just north of the lighthouse. Because there is a natural tendency for sand to wash away on the downdrift (southern) side of the groin, and because there is no fourth barrier to the south, the energy of storm-driven waves cuts in and around the southwest side of the tower. Thus, following severe storms, the southernmost groin has brought about the emergency erosion conditions that threaten the lighthouse.

In early 1999 a final attempt to halt the move was made by local county officials and residents. A petition for a motion for a preliminary injunction against the Department of Interior and the National Park Service to halt the relocation was submitted by the commissioners of Dare County and three property owners in March 1999 to federal judge Terrence Boyle of North Carolina's Fifth District.

At the time of the initial injunction hearing on March 15, the relocation process was already well underway. The front stairway to the tower, the original brick sidewalks, two underground freshwater cisterns, the brick oil house, and the double keepers quarters had already been moved to the new site. An access road, part of the move corridor, had been cleared, graded, proof-rolled, and graveled. And half of the lighthouse's granite stone foundation had been cored and mined; almost a third of the stone had been removed and replaced by shoring towers.

Judge Boyle considered the motion for two weeks and announced an initial ruling on April 2, Good Friday. He denied the motion to stop the move. Boyle concluded his public statement by noting, "The plaintiffs are unable to demonstrate that any of the four factors needed to support the issuance of a preliminary injunction were met." The plaintiffs later withdrew their filing. The way had been cleared for the uninterrupted relocation of Stetson's tower, well away from the danger of erosion.

Because International Chimney Corporation had been awarded both the planning and the construction phases of the

Relocation of the Cape Hatteras Light Station began in early 1999. Like sliding pieces of a puzzle into place, the 1871 principal keepers quarters was carefully moved to the new site. The double-brick walls of this house made it a sturdy structure that moved easily. There is archival evidence that originally the house was to have been a wooden structure, but the lighthouse construction foreman, Dexter Stetson, substituted leftover brick from the tower construction. The building is noted for its gingerbread appearance.

move process, planning sessions continued into the construction phase. Structural studies and detailed planning meetings had begun as early as July 1998. Site work began in December 1998 when truckloads of materials began arriving at the Cape Hatteras Light Station to prepare the tower and its outbuildings for the new site twenty-nine hundred feet southwest of the present site. A security fence was erected before the preparatory work commenced. Naturally, thousands of curious onlookers came to catch a glimpse of the beginning of the intricate process of moving the nation's most famous lighthouse.

As a result of the planning phase, the steps of the relocation were broken down into the following: The brick oil house, cisterns, and granite fence footers for an iron fence that once surrounded the lighthouse were to be moved first to clear an uninterrupted path for the keepers dwellings and the Stetson tower. The move corridor—the path down which the lighthouse would travel to reach its new foundation—would be cleared, graded, proofrolled, and compacted.

The chimneys and doorways on both the double and the principal keepers quarters would be braced. Since the freshwater water table is only four feet below ground, pumps would be installed to de-water the foundation area. While the foundation was sup-

While the keepers quarters were being moved, workers began the groundwork for the new lighthouse foundation. Below, two power shovels excavate the sixty-foot-square area for the new foundation. Four feet of seamless concrete are to be poured here and around a seventy-foot-square steel-beam mat to create a substantial support for the lighthouse tower.

The 1854 double keepers quarters was moved on February 23, 1999. Movers braced chimneys, lower-level windows, and doorways in preparation for the move. Lifted by main beams with built-in jacks, the quarters moved smoothly along the move path on aircraft-sized tires.

ported on temporary shoring (for example, oak cribbing and screw jacks), main beams would be placed under the houses with hydraulic jacks and cross steel. Each jack would be pressurized, locked off, and activated through "unified hydraulics." This technique allows all jacks to lift all parts of a structure at the same time, at the same rate. The lighthouse would be moved on steel rails or tracks, but the keepers quarters would be moved by rubber-tired dollies using aircraft-sized tires and a hydraulic assembly.

While en route to their new foundations the keepers quarters and the tower would be cushioned on hydraulics rigged under common pressure along three zones. This technique employs the basic geometric principle that three points determine a plane. A dip or rise along the move route could be accommodated by the three-zone principle, allowing for a compensation of pressures between hydraulic zones to keep the support system and thus the structures on a uniform, level plane.

Sensors would be installed on the lighthouse tower to monitor weather, acceleration, stress, and tilt. Two-by-fours would brace the sills in the lantern room and other obvious points, such as windows and the entryway. A scaling ladder would be rigged on the outside of the lighthouse all the way to the gallery deck. The tower's brickwork

At the relocation site, workers prepare the foundations for the two keeper quarters. The buildings will be placed in positions relative to their original construction, maintaining the same distances between each other and the lighthouse and the sea as they enjoyed when they were first built almost 130 years ago.

105

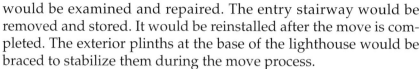
On February 13, 1999, the first cut was made on the lighthouse's granite foundation by the world's largest diamond-cable saw. Two days later the workers uncovered this century's first look at the pine-timber mat supporting the foundation of the lighthouse. Three layers of yellow pine lay in a grid formation on top of compacted sand below the fresh water table. Six pieces were removed from the section supporting the front step of the lighthouse for research purposes and a future display by the National Park Service.

would be examined and repaired. The entry stairway would be removed and stored. It would be reinstalled after the move is completed. The exterior plinths at the base of the lighthouse would be braced to stabilize them during the move process.

To excavate the present foundation, water would be removed from around the lighthouse. The tower's perimeter would be unearthed to a depth of about six feet. Enough water would remain over the pine timber mat supporting the foundation so as not to limit its exposure to air and prevent its deterioration. A diamond cable would separate the lighthouse from its granite foundation. The cut would be positioned between the first and second plinths, because the second through the fifth stepped, eight-sided granite plinths are above ground level and the first is below ground level. The outside perimeter stone units of the first plinth would be match-marked, removed, and stored until after the move. The movers would carefully mark any part of the historic structure to be removed so it could be replaced once the tower was repositioned at the new site.

Almost one thousand tons of foundation granite would be removed by coring, mining, and shoring the rock spans simultaneously over several weeks. Using hydraulic stone-cutting chainsaws, core drills, rock drills and hard splitters, the crew would focus on a single two- to four-foot swath at a time. Rock would be pulled or lifted out of place with an all-terrain forktruck.

As the rock is removed, temporary shoring would be set up in its place. The plan would be to work with small areas to remove the stone and then support the adjacent rock, opening localized areas until the pine timber mat is reached. As the space opens up, steel beams would be laid over the timber mat and welded together. Since the mat has been under water for 130 years and should be "springy" when the weight of the foundation is removed, the steel beams become a solid layer across which the load of the transport system and tower can be evenly spread.

While this excavation is going on, the weight of the tower will be borne by six-by-six oak cribbing and several shoring towers made of four individual steel posts bolted together laterally. Jacks are built into each shoring post along with a base plate to spread the load on the steel beam

mat. The jacks will push down on the mat and then be locked off, adding additional strength to the temporary support. A layer of shoring beams will be placed atop the shoring towers to evenly distribute the weight of the tower to the shoring towers.

The coring, mining, and shoring steps will be repeated until the lighthouse rests completely on the oak cribbing and shoring towers. As parts of the foundation are removed, additional beams will be added and pressurized to avoid edge-loading (as opposed to spread-loading) the shoring towers.

The time involved in this phase depends on the weather and how long it takes to remove the foundation stone. For safety's sake, whatever delays may occur can be as lengthy as the crew determines necessary. Plans project a time frame of ten to twelve weeks to install the temporary support system.

Once the support system is in place, steel main beams will be threaded between the shoring towers. They will be laid so as to point toward the direction of the move, underneath and perpendicular to the shoring beams. The main steel beam assembly will consist of duplex flanged steel beams welded together with built-in, heavy-duty hydraulic jacks. Base plates for the jacks will be

In the photograph on the left, the workmen erect the temporary support system integral to lifting the lighthouse tower from its granite foundation. The first complete section of the temporary support system is shown in the photograph on the right. Once the support system is in place, the granite foundation will be removed and the tower will rest entirely on these steel beams. At that point, a series of steel beams with built-in jacks will be threaded through the openings between the shoring tower posts to lift the lighthouse. It will then be pushed along another series of steel beams until it reaches its new foundation.

In this view of the move corridor, the path down which all the buildings of the light station will travel, the double keepers quarters can be seen already at the relocation site. When all the buildings are in place, the new site will duplicate the original appearance of the 1870 light station. Visitors to the compound will be able to view the historic district as it appeared when it was first operational.

laid under the jacks and will sit directly on the steel-beam mat that covers the foundation's pine-timber mat. Steel crossbeams will be placed over and perpendicular to the main steel and clamped to the main beams.

At this point the layers of material supporting the tower will be the original pine timber mat, the steel-beam mat, the shoring towers and the oak cribbing with beams threaded between them, a layer of shoring beams and crossbeams, and the base of lighthouse tower itself. Needle beams will be installed underneath the shoring beams and between the cross steel to support the individual stones that may be between the steel crossbeams. The hydraulic jacks will be activated then. When all jacks are pressurized correctly, according to the weight they support, an operator will activate the main unifying valve. The lighthouse will be lifted as a single unit a foot at a time. The jacks will be locked off individually to maintain the support pressure, and safety blocks will be installed. Cribbing will be added to equal the height of the lift. The newly cribbed jacks will then be repressurized, and the structure will be lifted the next foot. This procedure will be repeated until the lighthouse is six feet above ground and may take between one and two weeks.

The first several hundred feet of the move corridor will be carpeted with a mat of steel beams. At the excavation of the tower, these beams will overlay each other until they are the same height as the base of the lifted lighthouse. Oak-cribbing towers will fill in the gap between the steel mat in the corridor and the roll beams that will be extended to reach the move path.

While the main beams will be supported on the oak cribbing and the shoring posts, the jacks in each main beam will be depressurized and retracted, and a roll beam will be installed under them. The roll beams will have hardened-steel topside tracks to carry the weight of the lighthouse. Once in place, roller dollies will be installed alongside the hydraulic jacks. The jacks will then be pressurized and locked off. Shoring posts will be reset next to the main beams until the load of the lighthouse has been transferred

108

to the cribbed transportation system: main beams and jacks on roller dollies supported by roll beams.

Push jacks will be positioned behind the lighthouse, between the roll beams and the main beams. These jacks will be coordinated through the unified hydraulic system, pushing the lighthouse tower slowly, almost indiscernibly on the roller dollies along the travel beams. A dry lubricant will be used on the roll beams to ease the lighthouse across the track five or six feet at a time.

When the push jacks have reached their limit, the roll beams will be taken up from behind the tower and placed in front, thus recharging the system. When the roll beams are in place, the next push will be activated. If there are no delays, the process should take about six weeks.

International Chimney's engineers claim that the tower should be able to withstand winds over one hundred miles per hour while it is elevated during the move. Thus if a storm should hit while the move is underway, they say, the tower should not be at risk of falling over.

As an additional safety precaution, the steel mat in the move corridor will be laid about one foot below ground level for the first one hundred feet of the move. Should a storm cause any overwash, the sand will tend to fill in around the track rather than wash out from beneath it. Beyond the first 850 feet, each time the track system is recharged, the steel beam corridor mat will also be moved along with the travel beams to support the next push toward the relocation site.

The new lighthouse foundation will be a sixty-by-sixty-foot, four-foot-thick concrete pad resting on a foot-thick layer of stone. As the lighthouse nears its new foundation, the steel-beam matting will be stairstepped down level with the slab. The process of transferring the load onto the new foundation will reverse the sequence employed to lift the tower from its original foundation. The new site is higher than the original foundation and twenty-nine hundred feet away.

Once the tower is on its new foundation, the steel support system will be

As seen in this bird's-eye view of the lighthouse and the surrounding work area, the movers have little room to spare for the equipment necessary to accomplish the move.

removed section by section. Shoring towers will again be assembled around the base as a temporary support. An additional five feet of concrete will be poured onto the slab, infilling all open spaces under the foundation, and the shoring towers and transportation will be removed. In the end, the lighthouse tower will have a twelve-foot-deep foundation, giving the tower its most secure footing ever. By extending the diameter of the foundation from forty-eight feet to approximately seventy feet, because the steel reinforcement will extend beyond the concrete pad, the load of the tower will be more evenly distributed, giving it greater stability.

The lighthouse's new location, to be gained during the summer of 1999, will place it about sixteen hundred feet from the ocean—the same distance from the sea as when the Stetson tower was completed in 1870. The original pine-timber mat and remnants of the old stone foundation will remain in place, forever marking the 1870 site. Scientists say the new site will ensure the light's continued survival for the next century.

Thanks to the relocation process, the Cape Hatteras Light Station will look much as it did in the last sunset rays of the nineteenth century. It is now destined to greet the twenty-first century as a trophy for those who believe this National Historic Landmark should continue as a source of inspiration and imagination to many. The relocation promises many more years to share the story of the U.S. Lighthouse Service with generations who have never known of this maritime heritage.

APPENDIX

THE KEEPERS OF CAPE HATTERAS LIGHTHOUSE

Date Assumed Position	Name	Position Held	Date Departed
December 29, 1802	Adam Gaskins	Keeper	1808
1808	Joseph Farrow	Keeper	
March/April 1821	Pharoah Farrow	Keeper (?)	
November 25, 1830	Isaac S. Farrow	Keeper	December 1842
January 6, 1843	Joseph C. Jennett	Keeper	
?	Benjamin Fulcher	Keeper	May 23, 1849
1849	Hezekiah F. Farnett (Barnett)	Interim Keeper	1849
May 23, 1849	Joseph C. Jennett	Keeper	
July 7, 1853	William O'Neal	Keeper	July 9, 1860
April 7, 1854	H. B. O'Neal	1st Assistant	
April 7, 1854	W. B. O'Neal	1st Assistant	
January 23, 1855	R. Scarborough	1st Assistant	
October 30, 1856	E. D. Neal	1st Assistant	October 18, 1860
January 1, 1858	C. Fulcher	1st Assistant	?
June 9, 1860	E. F. O'Neal	Keeper	October 16, 1860
June 9, 1860	William Jennett	1st Assistant	October 16, 1860
October 16, 1860	Andrew Williams	Assistant	
October 16, 1860	B. A. Williams	Assistant	September 7, 1865
October 16, 1860	B. T. Fulcher	Keeper	
September 30, 1862	Abraham C. Farrow	Keeper	April 30, 1864
July 18, 1863	Wallace R. Jennett	Assistant	September 7, 1865
February 15, 1864	N. T. S. Williams	Assistant	April 10, 1871
March 2, 1864	Sylvester Robinson	Assistant	
April 14, 1864	George W. Rodgers	Keeper	August 16, 1866
December 22, 1864	L. B. Farrow	Assistant	January 23, 1867
September 7, 1865	Christopher A. Fulcher	Assistant	January 15, 1869
September 7, 1865	Abner H. Gray	Assistant	
August 16, 1866	Alpheus W. Simpson	Keeper	September 30, 1868
January 23, 1867	William B. O'Neal	Assistant	February/March 18, 1867

In the rare photograph of a keeper of the Cape Hatteras Lighthouse (right), assistant keeper James Oliver Casey posed in his Lighthouse Service uniform in early 1928.

Date Assumed Position	Name	Position Held	Date Departed
March 18, 1867	Wallace R. Jennett	Assistant	April 13, 1867
September 30, 1868	Benjamin C. Jennett	Keeper	March 18, 1871
September 30, 1868	Amassa Simpson Jr.	1st Assistant	
January 15, 1869	Joseph E. Jennett	Assistant	March 29, 1869
March 29, 1869	Alpheus W. Simpson Sr.	Assistant	April 13, 1869
April 13, 1869	C. P. Farrow	Assistant	June 29, 1871
April 11, 1870	Zion B. Jennett	Assistant	October 28, 1870
October 28, 1870	Nasa S. Williams	Assistant	
March 15, 1871	John W. Shepperd	Keeper	
June 29, 1871	Louis C. Roach	Assistant	
September 1875	Harry L. Farron	2d Assistant	
September 1875	Oliver N. Barnett	(Beacon Light)	
September 27, 1876	Alpheus W. Simpson	1st Assistant	
October 13, 1877	A. G. B. Salter	2d Assistant	June 11, 1888
September 1877	Ethelburt D. Burns	1st Assistant	
December 11, 1877	Oscar F. Rue	Acting Keeper	
April 1, 1878	Tilman F. Smith	3d Assistant	December 17, 1879
April 24, 1878	Oscar F. Rue	Keeper	July 15, 1880
July 22, 1878	Joseph B. Whitehurst	Assistant	
July 22, 1878	Alpheus W. Simpson	Assistant	
November 19, 1878	Tilman F. Smith	2d Assistant	
November 30, 1878	Selwyn Hause (House?)	Assistant	
April 17, 1879	John E. Whitehurst	Assistant	
December 18, 1879	Tilman F. Smith	1st Assistant	January 6, 1887
December 18, 1879	John E. Whitehurst	Assistant	
August 21, 1880	George A. Blivens	Keeper	January 5, 1881
January 6, 1881	Agustus C. Thompson	Keeper	January 6, 1887
December 13, 1883	A. J. Simpson	3d Assistant	June 2, 1883

Date Assumed Position	Name	Position Held	Date Departed
June 23, 1884	Fabius E. Simpson	3d Assistant	June 15, 1885
July 6, 1885	Wesley Austin	3d Assistant	January 11, 1889
September 1, 1885	David Willis	2d Assistant	January 6, 1887
January 7, 1887	Tilman F. Smith	Keeper	December 5, 1897
January 7, 1887	David Willis	1st Assistant	September 30, 1887
February 1, 1887	Christopher C. Miller	2d Assistant	September 30, 1887
October 1, 1887	Christopher C. Miller	1st Assistant	April 8, 1892
June 12, 1888	Louis G. Daniels	2d Assistant	January 11, 1889
January 12, 1889	Wesley Austin	2d Assistant	April 8, 1892
January 18, 1889	Ephraim H. Riggs	3d Assistant	April 8, 1892
April 1, 1892	Wesley Austin	1st Assistant	November 14, 1893
April 9, 1892	Ephraim H. Riggs	2d Assistant	June 9, 1892
April 15, 1892	Joseph B. Daniels	3d Assistant	June 16, 1892
June 17, 1892	Joseph B. Daniels	2d Assistant	November 14, 1893
July 28, 1892	Sanders B. Smith	3d Assistant	November 17, 1893
November 15, 1893	Sanders B. Smith	2d Assistant	December 31, 1899
November 17, 1893	Fabius E. Simpson	1st Assistant	December 31, 1899
January 13, 1894	Alpheus W. Simpson	3d Assistant	May 16, 1899
December 6, 1897	J. Wilson Gillikin	Keeper	May 31/June 1, 1900
June 7, 1899	John B. Jennett	3d Assistant	March 5, 1903
January 1, 1900	Martin G. Fulcher	2d Assistant	April 4, 1905
January 1, 1900	Sanders B. Smith	1st Assistant	March 5, 1903
June 1, 1900	Ephraim Meekins Jr.	Keeper	September 30, 1906
March 10, 1903	Amasa Fulcher	3d Assistant	March 31, 1904
April 1, 1904	John B. Quidley	3d Assistant	October 15, 1905
December 12, 1904	Joseph Farrow	Keeper	
January 22, 1905	Hezekiah F. Farnett (Barnett?)	Interim Keeper	
April 1, 1905	W. G. Falsom (Folsom?)	2d Assistant	April 15, 1905
April 10, 1905	Thomas H. Baum	1st Assistant	December 1, 1905
April 10, 1905	Isaac C. Meekins	2d Assistant	April 1, 1906
April 27, 1905	A. W. Tolson	Assistant	
October 16, 1905	William G. Rollinson (Robinson?)	3d Assistant	January 11, 1906
December 1, 1905	Alpheus B. Willis	1st Assistant	May 20, 1907

Light stations were often in remote areas far from medical help. For minor health problems or for emergency treatment until a doctor came, each station was equipped with a medicine chest like the one pictured here. The principal keeper was responsible for dispensing these medications or appointed a trustworthy assistant. These lotions, potions, and pills included sweet spirits of nitre (for colds and flatulence), arnica (for sprains and bruises), essence of Jamaica ginger quinine, cough mixtures, Rochelle salts and Senna leaves (a laxative), Castor oil (a purgative), carbolated oil and laudanum (antiseptics), glycerine (skin lotion), chloroform liniment, Lactopeptin. saltpeter, sulfur, quinine pills, cathartic pills, laudanum, carbolic acid, Iodoform (an antiseptic), opium and camphor pills (for general pain), "Dover's powders," and "Spirits camphor" (smelling salts).

Date Assumed Position	Name	Position Held	Date Departed
April 1, 1906	Charles H. Fulcher	2d Assistant	July 31, 1912
October 1, 1906	Fabius E. Simpson	Keeper	February 28, 1919
May 21, 1907	Jabez W. Burfoot	1st Assistant	October 23, 1907
October 24, 1907	Victor L. Watson	1st Assistant	September 30, 1909
October 3, 1909	Miles F. Whedbee	1st Assistant	October 10, 1909
October 16, 1909	John B. Quidley	1st Assistant	March 31, 1911
April 24, 1911	Alpheus B. Willis	1st Assistant	September 30, 1912
August 1, 1912	Homer T. Austin	2d Assistant	August 30, 1913
August 1, 1912	Charles H. Fulcher	1st Assistant	August 15, 1920
September 1, 1913	Malachi D. Swain	2d Assistant	April 13, 1917
May 16, 1917	John D. Brady	2d Assistant	August 10, 1917
August 20, 1917	Amasa J. Quidley	2d Assistant	September 30, 1923
March 16, 1919	Unaka B. Jennette	Keeper	1937
August 16, 1920	James O. Casey	1st Assistant	February 28, 1928
October 1, 1923	William E. Quidley	2d Assistant	August 15, 1928
April 1, 1928	Randolph P. Fulcher	1st Assistant	August 8, 1928
August 16, 1928	William E. Quidley	1st Assistant	September 30, 1934
September 1, 1928	Julian H. Austin	2d Assistant	March 31, 1929
April 1, 1929	John E. Midgett	2d Assistant	October 31, 1930
November 1, 1930	John M. Stowe	2d Assistant	November 2, 1931
November 3, 1931	Thomas L. Wallace	2d Assistant	September 14, 1933

NOTES:

- Keeper indicates Principal Keeper

- 3d assistant keeper position abolished in January 1906, probably due to the demise of the Cape Point Beacon, which had been the primary responsibility of the 3d assistant keeper.

- 2d assistant keeper position abolished on September 14, 1933, and 1st assistant keeper position abolished on August 1, 1934, probably due to the installation of electricity at the Cape Hatteras Light Station in 1934. Electricity provided a much more reliable light source, which decreased the need for a keeper standing watch. The electric light also eliminated the need of cleaning soot from the lens.

SOURCES:

This list was compiled from available records, including the National Archives, the National Park Service, U.S. Lighthouse Service, Ross Holland, Charlie Votaw, and Sandy Clunies. A fire in Baltimore in 1904 and a fire at the U.S. Commerce Department in the 1920s destroyed many of the nineteenth- and early twentieth-century Lighthouse Service records, which makes it difficult to verify names and dates of service.

BIBLIOGRAPHY

Adams, W. H. Davenport. *Lighthouses and Lightships.* London: T. Nelson and Sons, 1870.

Bloomfield, Howard V. L. *The Compact History of the United States Coast Guard: The Story of the American Coast Guardsman and the Force in Which He Serves.* New York: Hawthorn Books, 1966.

Browning, Robert (historian, U.S. Coast Guard, Washington, D.C.). Interview by Shelton-Roberts, October 1998.

Bureau of Lighthouses. *U.S. Lighthouse Service Bulletins.* Washington, D.C.: Government Printing Office, 1912–39.

Carr, Dawson. *The Cape Hatteras Lighthouse: Sentinel of the Shores.* Chapel Hill: University of North Carolina Press, 1991.

Crawford, William P. *Mariner's Notebook.* San Francisco: Miller Freeman Publications, 1971.

Crowninshield, Mary Bradford. *All Among the Lighthouses.* Boston: D. Lothrop and Co., 1886.

Cutter, William Richard. *Genealogical and Personal Memoirs Relating to the Families of Boston and Eastern Massachusetts.* New York: Lewis Historical Publishing Co., 1908.

DeBlieu, Jan. *Hatteras Journal.* Golden, Colo.: Fulcrum, 1987; reprint, Winston-Salem, N.C.: J. F. Blair, 1998.

Eldridge, James. *History of the Cape Hatteras Light Station.* Washington, D.C.: National Park Service, 1954.

Eshelman, Ralph E., and Candace Clifford. "National Register of Historic Places Registration," nomination papers. National Park Service, National Maritime Initiative (NRHE 2280), Washington, D.C. July 26, 1997.

Fowler, William M., Jr. *Under Two Flags: The American Navy in the Civil War.* New York: Avon Books, 1990.

Fresnel, Augustin. Papers. Ambassade de France aux Etats-Unis, Service de Presse et d'Information, Washington, D.C.

Friesen, Pete (consultant for hard-to-move objects, retired). Interview by Shelton-Roberts, January 1999.

Gannon, Michael. *Operation Drumbeat.* New York: HarperPerennial, 1991.

Gibbs, Myrtle Jennette (daughter of Cape Hatteras principal keeper Unaka Jennette). Interview by Shelton-Roberts, January 1999.

Gray, Charles. *Data on Efforts of the U.S. Government to Establish and Maintain a Lighthouse at Cape Hatteras.* Washington, D.C.: National Park Service, 1938.

Guindon, Ed (artist, International Chimney Corporation). Interview by Shelton-Roberts, December 1998.

Hart, Charles and Sons. "Lighthouse for Outer Diamond Shoal Off Cape Hatteras, NC." New York. Supplemental to *Engineering News* (1890).

Heap, Major D. P. "Ancient and Modern Light-Houses." 1889. Reprint, Nautical Research Centre (1991).

Hickam, Homer H., Jr. *Torpedo Junction.* Annapolis: Naval Institute Press, 1989.

Hill, Daniel Harvey. *Bethel to Sharpsburg.* Raleigh: Edwards and Broughton Co., 1926.

Holland, F. Ross, Jr. (National Park Service Historian, retired). *A History of Cape Hatteras Light Station.* Washington, D.C.: Division of History, National Park Service, 1968.

———. Interview by Shelton-Roberts, January 1999.

———. *Keeper's Dwelling: Cape Hatteras Light Station.* Washington, D.C.: Division of History, National Park Service, 1968.

Hyde, Charles K. *The Northern Lights: Lighthouses of the Upper Great Lakes.* Lansing: Two Peninsula Press, 1986.

Jakubik, Joe. International Chimney Corporation. Interviews by Shelton-Roberts, 1995–99.

Johnson, Robert Erwin. *Guardians of the Sea: History of the United States Coast Guard 1915 to the Present.* Annapolis: Naval Institute Press, 1987.

Kendall, Connie Jo. "Let There Be Light: The History of Lighthouse Illuminants." *The Keeper's Log,* 13, no. 3 (1997): 22–29.

King, Edith (daughter of last commissioner of lighthouses). Interviews by Shelton-Roberts, 1997–98.

Light-House Board. *Instructions to Light-Keepers.* 1902. Reprint, Allen Park: Great Lakes Lighthouse Keepers Association, 1989.

———. *Instructions to Light-Keepers.* Washington, D.C.: 1881, 1893, 1902, 1928.

116

Livingston, Dewey, and Dave Snow. *The History and Architecture of the Point Reyes Light Station.* Washington, D.C.: National Park Service, 1990.

McComb, John. "Estimate for Building a Lighthouse on Cape Hatteras in North Carolina." 1797.

Matyiko, Jim (Expert House Movers). Interview by Shelton-Roberts, November 1998.

Moore, Frank. *The Rebellion Record: A Diary of American Events.* 11 vols. New York: G. P. Putnam, 1862. Vols. 3 and 4.

Move the Lighthouse Committee. "Move It or Lose It! The Case for Relocation of Cape Hatteras Lighthouse." Cary, N.C.: Move the Lighthouse Committee, 1987.

Munn and Company, eds. "Proposed Lighthouse for Cape Hatteras Diamond Shoal." *Scientific American,* July 11, 1904, 462.

Noble, Dennis. *Lighthouses and Keepers: The U.S. Lighthouse Service and Its Legacy.* Annapolis: Navy Institute Press, 1997.

North Carolina State University. *Saving the Cape Hatteras Lighthouse from the Sea.* Raleigh: North Carolina State University, 1997.

Parker, William Harwar. *Recollections of a Naval Officer, 1841–1865.* New York: Charles Scribner's Sons, 1885.

Patterson, Stanley C., and Carl G. Seaburg. *Nahant on the Rocks.* Nahant, Mass.: Nahant Historical Society, 1991.

Pilkey, Orrin H., et al. *The North Carolina Shore and Its Barrier Islands.* Durham and London: Duke University Press, 1998.

Porter, Charles W. *A Field Investigation at Cape Hatteras Lighthouse.* National Park Service Report. Washington, D.C.: Government Printing Office, 1938.

Putman, George R. "Beacons of the Sea: Lighting the Coast of the United States." *National Geographic Magazine* (January 1913): 1–53.

———. *Sentinel of the Coast, Log of a Lighthouse Engineer.* New York: W. W. Norton & Company, 1937.

Roberts, Bruce, and Ray Jones. *Southeastern Lighthouses.* Old Saybrook, Conn.: Globe Pequot Press, 1994.

Sears, Calanthas (Nahant, Massachusetts, Historical Society, historian). Interview by Shelton-Roberts, February 1999.

Shelton-Roberts, Cheryl. "Master C. C. Austin Saves Diamond Shoals Lightship during Hurricane of 1933." *Lighthouse News* 3, no. 4 (1997).

———. "Cape Hatteras: Last Family Member Leaves the Lighthouse." *Lighthouse News* 2, no. 2 (1995).

———. "Light Years Away." *Lighthouse News* 2, no. 1 (1996).

———, and Bruce Roberts. *Lighthouse Families.* Birmingham, Ala.: Crane Hill Publishers, 1997.

Stackpole, Everett S. *History of Durham, Maine with Genealogical Notes.* Lewiston, Maine: Lewiston Journal Co., 1899.

Stick, David. *Graveyard of the Atlantic.* Chapel Hill: University of North Carolina Press, 1952.

———. *North Carolina Lighthouses.* Raleigh: Division of Archives and History, North Carolina Department of Cultural Resources, 1992.

———. *The Outer Banks of North Carolina.* Chapel Hill: University of North Carolina Press, 1958.

Tag, Thomas (expert on lamps, lighting apparatus, and lenses). Interview by Shelton-Roberts, January 1999.

Talbot, Frederick A. *Lightships and Lighthouses.* Philadelphia: J. B. Lippincott Co., 1913.

Torres, Louis. *Historic Resource Study of Cape Hatteras National Seashore.* Denver: National Park Service, n.d.

U.S. Bureau of the Census. Records 1870 for Dare County. Division of Archives and History, Raleigh, N.C.

U.S. Coast Guard. *Cape Hatteras Lighthouse, North Carolina Fourth Groin Alternative Design Report and Environmental Assessment.* Wilmington, N.C., 1996.

———. Various internal communications and memoranda, 1941–1950.

U.S. Congress. Third Congress of the United States. An Act to Erect a Lighthouse on the Head-Land of Cape Hatteras. Philadelphia, 1793.

U.S. Department of the Interior. "Application for National Historic Landmark Nomination: Cape Hatteras Light Station." Washington, D.C.: National Park Service, 1998.

———. Various National Park Service internal communications and memoranda, 1936–1950.

U.S. Light-House Board. *Annual Reports of Light-House Board.* Washington, D.C.: Government Printing Office, 1872, 1890, 1903, 1914, 1917, 1918, 1928. 1935, 1936, 1937, 1938, 1939, 1939, 1940. (This material was later published as volume 1, no. 1 of *Coast Guard Bulletin.*)

———. *Report of the Officers Constituting the Light-House Board.* Washington, D.C.: Government Printing Office, 1852.

U.S. Lighthouse Service. *Encroachment of Sea: Cape Hatteras Light Station.* Washington, D.C.: Government Printing Office, 1919.

————. *List of Beacons, Buoys, and Day-Marks in the Fifth Light-House District.* Washington, D.C.: Government Printing Office, 1854–1904.

Wallace, David H. *Principal Keeper's Quarters Cape Hatteras Light Station.* Harpers Ferry Center: National Park Service, 1991.

Warren, Edward. *A Doctor's Experiences in Three Continents.* Baltimore: Cushings & Bailey, 1885.

Weiss, George. *The Lighthouse Service: Its History, Activities, and Organization.* Baltimore: Johns Hopkins Press, 1926.

Wentworth, Margaret (Durham, Maine, Historical Society, historian). Interview by Shelton-Roberts, February 1999.

Whitney, Dudley. *The Lighthouse.* Boston: New York Graphic Society, 1975.

Wilson, Fred A. *Some Annals of Nahant Massachusetts.* Boston: Old Corner Book Store, 1928.

Woodward, R. M. *Prevention of Disease and Care of the Sick and Injured: Medical Handbook for the Use of Lighthouse Vessels and Stations.* Washington: Lighthouse Service, 1915.

Woody, Robert E. (National Park Service, Cape Hatteras, chief of planning and partnerships). Interviews by Shelton-Roberts, October-December, 1998.

CREDITS

Page ii: National Archives. *Page vii:* National Archives. *Page xv:* Bruce Roberts. *Page xviii:* Bruce Roberts. *Page 6:* Bruce Roberts. *Page 7:* Bruce Roberts. *Page 10:* W. H. Davenport Adams, *Lighthouses and Lightships* (London: T. Nelson and Sons, 1870), 75. *Page 11:* Outer Banks History Center. *Page 12:* Outer Banks History Center. *Page 17:* (all) Library of Congress. *Page 18:* (left) Thomas A. Tag; (right) Outer Banks History Center. *Page 19:* (both) Mary Bradford Crowninshield, *All Among the Lighthouses* (Boston: D. Lothrop and Co., 1886), 43. *Page 20:* Outer Banks History Center. *Page 24:* North Carolina Archives and History. *Page 35:* (both) National Archives. *Page 36:* (both) National Archives. *Page 37:* National Archives. *Page 38:* Outer Banks History Center. *Page 39:* Outer Banks History Center. *Page 41:* U.S. Coast Guard Archives. *Page 45:* Nahant [Mass.] Historical Society. *Page 46:* Nahant [Mass.] Historical Society. *Page 47:* Nahant [Mass.] Historical Society. *Page 48:* Bruce Roberts. *Page 49:* Auburn Public Library, Auburn, Maine. *Page 52:* Collection of Cheryl Roberts. *Page 53:* (both) Outer Banks History Center. *Page 54:* (all) National Archives. *Page 55: Scientific American,* June 11, 1904. *Page 56:* Outer Banks History Center. *Page 57:* Courtesy of U.S. Coast Guard. *Page 59:* Courtesy of U.S. Coast Guard. *Page 60:* Courtesy of U.S. Coast Guard. *Page 62:* Outer Banks History Center. *Page 63:* Outer Banks History Center. *Page 66:* Courtesy of Rany Jennette. *Page 68:* North Carolina Archives and History. *Page 69:* Outer Banks History Center. *Page 70:* National Park Service. *Page 73:* (all) Courtesy of Edith E. King. *Page 74:* (both) Outer Banks History Center. *Page 76:* Courtesy of the National Park Service. *Page 79:* Outer Banks History Center. *Page 80:* (all) Bruce Roberts. *Page 82:* (both) Bruce Roberts. *Page 84:* North Carolina History and Archives. *Page 85:* North Carolina History and Archives. *Page 90:* Outer Banks History Center. *Page 91:* Outer Banks History Center. *Page 92:* North Carolina History and Archives. *Page 93:* North Carolina History and Archives. *Page 94:* Courtesy of the National Park Service. *Page 95:* The Ray Couch Collection, Outer Banks History Center. *Page 96:* Courtesy of the National Park Service. *Page 97:* (both) Outer Banks History Center. *Page 98:* (top) Mike Litwin, (bottom) Outer Banks History Center. *Page 99:* Bruce Roberts. *Page 100:* Bruce Roberts. *Page 102:* Bruce Roberts. *Page 103:* Bruce Roberts. *Page 104:* (both) Bruce Roberts. *Page 105:* (both) Bruce Roberts. *Page 106:* Bruce Roberts. *Page 107:* (both) Bruce Roberts. *Page 108:* Bruce Roberts. *Page 109:* Bruce Roberts. *Page 112:* (left) National Archives, (right) courtesy of Jim Casey. *Color insert section:* all photographs by Bruce Roberts except for the image of the Fresnel lens at Pigeon Point, Calif., on page 8, which is reproduced courtesy of Nancy A. Pizzo. All artwork by Mike Litwin.

INDEX